P9-BZD-669

goodness

MICHAEL REDHILL

COACH HOUSE BOOKS

copyright © Michael Redhill, 2005

first edition

For production or music enquiries, please contact Pam Winter at the Gary Goddard Agency in Toronto: pamwintergga@bellnet.ca

 Canada Council for the Arts   Conseil des Arts du Canada   ONTARIO ARTS COUNCIL CONSEIL DES ARTS DE L'ONTARIO   Canadä

Published with the assistance of the Canada Council for the Arts and the Ontario Arts Council. We also acknowledge the Government of Canada through the Book Publishing Industry Development Program.

LIBRARY AND ARCHIVES CANADA CATALOGUING IN PUBLICATION

Redhill, Michael, 1966-
    Goodness / Michael Redhill. – 1st ed.

A play.
ISBN 1-55245-163-1

    1. Genocide–Drama. I. Title.

PS8585.E3425G66 200   C812'.54   C2005-906346-7

He drags me, he drags me away –
Do you not see? –
To the House of the Dead,
The Winged One

Alcestis, Euripedes

Szerelem, szerelem / átkozott gyötrelem
(Love, love / wretched suffering)

Hungarian folk song

Goodness premiered at Tarragon Theatre in Toronto on October 25, 2005, as a Volcano/Tarragon co-production, with the following cast and crew:

Victor Ertmanis	MATHIAS TODD, THERAPIST, POLE 3
Lili Francks	ALTHEA
Tara Hughes	YOUNG ALTHEA, POLE 1, VOICE, HELENA SONNEN
Jack Nicholsen	STEPHEN PART, COLIN, MAN, POLE 4
Jordan Pettle	MICHAEL REDHILL
Bernadeta Wrobel	JULIA TODD, JOANNA, POLE 2

Ross Manson	Director
Brenna MacCrimmon	Music Director
Teresa Pryzbylski	Set and Costume Design
Rebecca Picherack	Lighting Design
John Gzowski	Sound Design
JP Robichaud	Stage Manager

The characters in this play never leave the stage – the stage being an imaginative space in which Michael Redhill, the character, is writing the play. Other than Michael and Althea, the rest of the characters act as a kind of chorus – each has a primary character, but they take on other roles in a way that has a meaningful interaction with Michael's thoughts or Althea's memories.

Act One

Darkness onstage. Under this darkness, multiple voices.

SONG: '*Tobela*' (Zimbabwean)

Chorus:
Tobela Murena / Tobela Murena   (Pray to God)
Tobela Murena / Tobela Murena

Tobela Murena / Tobela Murena
Tobela Murena / Tobela Murena

Horiyatsa	(Look around / pay attention)
Hamuzani waka	(To what is happening)
Tobela	(Pray)
Ayitobela Murena	(O Pray to God)

Tobela Murena / Tobela Murena
Tobela Murena / Tobela Murena

Horiyatsa	(Look around / pay attention)
Hamuzani waka	(To what is happening)
Tobela	(Pray)
Ayitobela Murena	(O Pray to God)

Iyo-o / Iyo-o / Iyo-o	(a soothing sound)
Ayitobela Murena	(O Pray to God)

Lights up. There are six people onstage, five of whom – JULIA, STEPHEN, TODD, ALTHEA, YOUNG ALTHEA – are looking at MICHAEL, whose nose is buried in a notebook. He's writing. After a moment:

MICHAEL: (*remembering the music*) That was it. (*to us as well as the other five characters*) Sorry, I just have to get this down. (*He finishes, holds up the notebook.*) I'm trying to write a play ... although, if you can hear me, I guess it's finished.

Even though right now I could throw it through a window. (*pause, realizing*) You're sitting in a theatre at this very moment, aren't you? Somewhere, in the future, you're in a dark room, and it just got quiet, and you have no idea what's going to happen to you. You've paid your money, you're in your seat and … you're staring at the playwright. Although it's not me, I have to say. I'm being played tonight by Jordan Pettle. That's a little lie in the form of a person. You're in good hands with Jordan, by the way. He's an excellent actor, a trained actor, who's been in many Canadian plays of repute. You probably saw him in *Waiting for Godot*. A Jewish Estragon – imagine. *For Godot, We're Waiting*. But he was fantastic. So thank you, Jordan. You have my trust, and my gratitude.

Now, this is a true story. I want to be upfront about that. And I'm a real person. You can look me up in the Toronto Yellow Pages, under 'ghost writers': I write bumpf for corporations and pap for cash. But apart from myself there are real people in this play who probably don't know they're in it, and so I've changed their names. I don't strictly have their permission to write about them. Although I'm sure you won't have a problem with that – the reason *why* I've decided to. One of the people I'm referring to is my ex-wife –

Julia, as Joanna, tears the notebook from Michael's hands.

JOANNA (JULIA): What the hell do you think you're doing?

MICHAEL: My divorce was really the first domino to fall in a series of … I found out she was having an affair.

JOANNA: You read my diary?

MICHAEL: Oh, *you* feel betrayed?

JOANNA: I feel invaded.

MICHAEL: (*suddenly shouting*) YOU SLEPT WITH COLIN!

JOANNA: It figures you'd have to read someone else's diary to know what's going on in your own life.

MICHAEL: (*to us*) He was my best friend.

COLIN (STEPHEN): Hey pal.

MICHAEL: BACK OFF.

COLIN : (*to Michael*) Where do you get your ideas? (*Stephen, as Colin, laughs mildly. Then, as an aside to Julia*) Hi, hon – I put the laundry on the bed.

JOANNA: (*to Stephen*) Thanks, sweetie. (*She looks in Michael's book, then says, honestly*) 'Bumpf' and 'pap.' That's good. (*She hands him back the book.*) Am I going to be in your play? Your horrible ex-wife?

MICHAEL: No.

JOANNA: Prick. You got what you deserved.

She backs away with Stephen.

MICHAEL: I had a little depression after my breakup. Okay: I could barely move for eight months. I'd get up in the mornings but before I could make it to the bathroom, I'd have to lie down again. I grew a beard and got fat. My shrink said,

THERAPIST (TODD): How does it feel?

MICHAEL: How does it *feel*?

THERAPIST : You should get away from your life for a while. Focus on something else.

MICHAEL: Like what.

THERAPIST : Go on a trip. Try to have some fun.

MICHAEL: Where am I going to have 'fun'?

THERAPIST : Just go somewhere. Get away from yourself. God, you're depressing, you know that?

MICHAEL: (*to us*) He never really said that. Although he might as well have. Useless … Anyway, I took his advice.

Blackout.

SONG: '*Szerelem*' (Hungarian)

Szerelem szerelem	(Love, love)
Átkozott gyötrelem	(Wretched suffering)

Lights up. He turns the notebook to us. There are pictures taped to two pages.

MICHAEL: These are my mother's grandparents and seven of their children. All of them were killed in 1941, in the town square of Ustrzyki Dolne, in Poland, by the Einsatzgruppen. The Nazi death squads.
　　　Nine people.

SONG: *Szerelem szerelem*

So, this is what I did after my divorce. It probably seems crazy to you, but I went to Poland. Granted, my shrink didn't say, 'Sublimate your feelings of loss and worthlessness by making an Orphic journey to your family's tragic past' –

SONG: *Átkozott gyötrelem*

– but what the hell.

POLE 1 (YOUNG ALTHEA): No. It's *Oos Tshikee Dolnya*.

MICHAEL: *Oos Tshikee Dolnya.*

POLE 2 (JULIA): Tak. (*Ad lib in Polish along the lines of 'he says it with a Yiddish accent' – the Poles laugh*)

MICHAEL: It turned out the people I met in Poland weren't all that interested in my 'quest.'

POLE 3 (TODD): You think the Nazis came through just to make life hard for the Jews?

POLE 4 (STEPHEN): We had the Russki on one side and the Nazi on the other, and you come to Poland looking for bad guys!

POLE 2: (*In Polish: 'Who is this guy?'*)

POLE 1: The Lone Ranger.

The Poles laugh.

MICHAEL: (*suddenly furious*) HEY! There's no need to be so rude, tak?

POLE 2: Tak? Hey, chill man. We're just playing with you. C'mon, ask us anything. Honest.

He stares at them and they stare back. He turns away from them.

MICHAEL: These people weren't going to tell me anything, so I left. It was a mistake to go in the first place.

He turns away from them, is back in the shrink's office.

THERAPIST: Poland? You're planning a trip to Poland? Do you really think that's a good idea? I was thinking something more like Vegas.

MICHAEL: I hate Vegas.

THERAPIST: Let's talk about your ex-wife.

MICHAEL: Let's not.

THERAPIST: You marry a non-Jew, she leaves you for a non-Jew. Any connection here to the sudden interest in the history of your people?

MICHAEL: Oh. You mean am I displacing my anger at my gentile ex-wife by trying to take it out on a bunch of Jew-killing Poles?

THERAPIST: Are you?

MICHAEL: I know what I'm doing, okay?

SONG: '*Yonana*' (Zimbabwean)

Yonana yo yo yo
Yonana yo yo yo

Michael becomes aware of the audience again. He is thinking in circles.

Where were we? Yeah. Poland. I took a train from Warsaw through the green green fields to Berlin, and from there went to London to wait for my plane home. Annnnd ... you know what? That's the end of the play! Thank you for coming. Good night.

Blackout. Pause. The song returns, (Althea sings 'Yonana.' All join on 'Yo.') louder than before, more insistent. Lights up. Michael is suddenly in an English pub, with a man (Stephen) sitting beside him. The man speaks without an accent.

MAN (STEPHEN): (*amused*) You went all the way to Poland and you thought they'd be happy to see you?

MICHAEL: I said: good night.

MAN: What the hell were you were doing there?

Michael is handed a drink. He looks at it.

MICHAEL: Fine. (*to the audience*) I had a few hours to kill in London before my flight. I met this old guy in some rundown –

MAN: You're lucky they didn't shoot you too.

MICHAEL: It was a little idealistic, maybe. (*Drinks, beat.*) Look, I knew it wouldn't be easy, but I didn't go with a chip on my shoulder. I –

MAN: Let me get this straight. You flew in from overseas, rented a Corolla in Warsaw and drove down to the Carpathian mountains to see if some old folks felt like admitting their part in unspeakable crimes against your people?

MICHAEL: No. I wasn't trying to get anyone to sign a confession. If you're really interested, I was trying to see how they experienced what happened there. Because our histories intersect.

MAN: Your histories don't 'intersect,' yours is a subplot of theirs.

MICHAEL: It's healthy to talk about what you've done.

MAN: Is it?

MICHAEL: Trust me. And it's been sixty years anyway.

MAN: Right. Sixty years of rubble and oppression and Communism. And *revolt*. And repression of the Catholics. And *corruption*. And *poverty*. And *industrial pollution*. And the Miracle of the Free Market! Jews? Holocaust?

MICHAEL: You're Polish.

MAN: Really? Do I look Polish?

MICHAEL: (*to us*) He didn't look Polish, but he might as well have been.

MAN: What?

MICHAEL: I wasn't talking to you.

The man looks out. Then back to Michael.

MAN: Listen, I'm not from your side of the ocean. We know history here like you Americans know cartoons.

MICHAEL: I'm Canadian actually.

MAN: Ah yes. (*quoting something*) 'The minority culture *is*, the majority culture *does*.'

MICHAEL: (*quoting the man*) 'Ah yes.' What the hell are you talking about?

MAN: Write it down. (*insistent, when Michael remains inactive*) Write it down!

Michael reluctantly opens the notebook.

MAN: While the Few expound on their uniqueness, the Many are figuring out how to get rid of them. (*He laughs, Michael closes the book.*) Listen, holocausts happen all the time. Really. Africa, the Caucasus, Europe, Cambodia. They're very popular, holocausts. Although most of the last, what, sixty have been completely forgotten. Except by the survivors who go around wailing and pointing their fingers, 'You! Go stand trial!, You! Go to the Hague!' and they try to punish us with the story over and over so we'll never forget! But you know what? Everyone has moved on. Except you. You had some bad luck, and you want everyone to pay.

MICHAEL: You call the Holocaust 'bad luck'? Where *are* you from?

MAN: Does it matter?

MICHAEL: When you talk like that it does.

MAN: Consider this. Let's say Hitler doesn't come to power –

MICHAEL: No, let's NOT say that.

MAN: – and Germany copes with the after-effects of the Great Depression some other way.

MICHAEL: So they lower the interest rates instead of, you know, gassing everybody.

MAN: Sure, let's say that.

MICHAEL: Please.

MAN: And everyone thrives. The Jews thrive as well, their numbers increase, they get a voice in government, and one day some of them say, 'The Aryans sure do have a lot of control of industry' –

MICHAEL: 'We should put limits on them!'

MAN: And one thing leads to another and before you know it, the Jews are rounding up the Germans and putting them on trains.

MICHAEL: Well, this is just like all the other times in history the Jews ran rampant and went around killing people, isn't it? Jesus Christ.

MAN: Right! Let's start with him.

MICHAEL: OH! (*to us*) Okay, fine, do you see? (*to man*) Now, THIS IS – this is *exactly* the reason why you people have so many bloody genocides over here! Because you'll find any reason at all to make a 'them' so you can be an 'us,' and then – *look!* – you've got micks and dagos and chinks and niggers and kikes who are corrupting your language and screwing your women and killing your gods! The whole, the whole *IDEA* that there might be some *likeness* between all human beings – well, that's *anathema*!

MAN: (*He's been watching the display.*) Oh, I like you.

MICHAEL: What?

MAN: You take it all so personally! It's refreshing.

MICHAEL: I'm not here to amuse you, bud.

MAN: No, you're an idealist. You think people should be held *accountable*!

MICHAEL: I came over here for a good reason.

MAN: Of course. (*Beat.*) What was that?

MICHAEL: I'm a survivor. I have a responsibility.

MAN: Yes, right. (*Beat.*) What did you survive again?

MICHAEL: (*getting up to leave*) Never mind.

MAN: No, no … no. Sit down. You were winning! You've met an uninformed old fool in a bar and you *stood your ground*. A lesser man walks out calling me an asshole, but you don't, you get your point across. Am I right?

MICHAEL: About what.

MAN: Some people are chosen. I know. The world is so full of idiots spouting their received wisdom, and some people see right through it. To the truth.

MICHAEL: And you're one of those people?

MAN: No. You are.

MICHAEL: (*Sits down.*) My wife left me for my best friend, and I just spent three thousand dollars to get laughed out of Poland. I don't think you're forming the right impression of me.

MAN: You're angry and betrayed and you want something to change.

MICHAEL: So what.

MAN: It can happen.

MICHAEL: I sincerely doubt that.

MAN: Ask me to make it happen.

MICHAEL: (*to us*) I was sitting there thinking, 'This is going to be good.' Me drinking alone, some crusty old guy with some kind of a problem and he doesn't even know he's talking to a writer.

MAN: (*Opens Michael's book.*) You got any blank pages in here?

MICHAEL: (*to man*) I'd rather if you –

MAN: You're some kind of writer, huh? (*He tears out a page; Michael flinches.*) This is the address of a friend of mine. Take her a message for me and she'll give you something you want.

MICHAEL: No thanks.

MAN: (*Gives up instantly.*) No? Okay.

Pause.

MICHAEL: Fine. Who is she.

MAN: Her name is –

MICHAEL: (*Michael stops the man from speaking.*) I'm calling her 'Althea.'

MAN: Althea. We worked together on a project once. In another place, but it didn't pan out.

MICHAEL: You want me to visit your ex.

MAN: Not quite.

MICHAEL: Then what?

MAN: She has something of mine. I need it back.

MICHAEL: She owes you money?

MAN: Not that.

MICHAEL: Why don't you go see her?

MAN: I'm not invited.

MICHAEL: And I am?

MAN: She'll like you.

He holds out the paper with the address on it. Michael doesn't take it.

MICHAEL: Hi there! I'm Michael. Some guy in a bar thinks you'll like me. Can I come in?

MAN: First, what you do is you apologize for disturbing her. You say you just want five minutes of her time. And when she says she doesn't have five minutes, you tell her a name. Mathias Todd.

MICHAEL: And that's you?

MAN: No. But you see, you say that name, she gets a message, and she opens the door.

MICHAEL: You really think I'm going to visit this woman, don't you?

MAN: Because you will.

MICHAEL: Uh, no I won't.

MAN: Well, you think you won't, but you will.

MICHAEL: You know what? You're an asshole.

MAN: And you'd be a fool to turn down your only opportunity to have your question answered.

MICHAEL: Oh, right. And what was my question?

MAN: Why do good people rush to do evil? And what do they become? (*Long beat.*) Think what a story that will make.

This freezes Michael.

SONG: '*Heyamo*' (a work song from the Black Sea area of Turkey)

> *He He Heyamo*   (Heyamo – a greeting, as in 'hello')

> (*The song goes on to say 'Your aunt is having a work party. It's time to start digging.'*)

MICHAEL: I didn't get your name.

MAN: I know.

SONG: *Yamo Hemo Heyamo*

> *The man stands up.*

MAN: Remember: 'Mathias Todd.' Tell her 'Mathias Todd.' She'll make Poland look like Disneyland.

SONG: *Heyamoli Heyamo*

> *The man holds the address out to Michael.*

MICHAEL: His fingernails were perfect white crescent moons.

MAN: Maybe you'll see me again.

> *The man drifts away.*

> '*Heyamo*' *is sung under the following, harmonies are added.*

MICHAEL: When I stepped outside, I realized the address he'd written down was across the street. This man must have been watching this woman coming and going … (*Beat.*) I had seven hours to catch my plane. I could have gone to a movie and had a nice long dinner somewhere, but …

Althea appears.

ALTHEA: Hello?

MICHAEL: I used the buzzcode the man had written down. There was music playing in the background.

ALTHEA: Hello?

MICHAEL: I didn't know what I was doing.

ALTHEA: Who is it!

MICHAEL: Um, it's uh, um, uh, my name's Michael.

ALTHEA: Who?

MICHAEL: Listen, someone, a friend of yours, suggested I come and talk to you.

ALTHEA: I don't have any friends.

MICHAEL: Well sure you do. Everyone has friends. (*Long beat.*) Hello? He asked me to give you a message. He told me to say 'Mathias Todd.'

ALTHEA: (*Beat.*) Are you a reporter?

MICHAEL: No, no – well, uh, I am a writer, but I'm not –

ALTHEA: How did you find me?

MICHAEL: I … A man – in a bar … gave me your … (*realizing how absurd this sounds*) Ohh boy.

ALTHEA: You're an American.

MICHAEL: No, Canadian. (*Beat.*) Sorry.

ALTHEA: Where in Canada.

MICHAEL: Toronto?

ALTHEA: Just a moment. (*Pause – she retreats into her apartment.*)

MICHAEL: Ma'am?

ALTHEA: What state is Toronto in, and what is the capital of that state?

MICHAEL: What?

ALTHEA: Answer.

MICHAEL: Toronto's in Ontario, which is a *province*, and it's also the capital. Of the province.

ALTHEA: No it isn't. I'm calling the police.

MICHAEL: WAIT WAIT, hold on! … Are you looking at an atlas?

ALTHEA: Yes. And Ottawa is the capital of Ontario.

MICHAEL: *No*, no – Ottawa, it's the capital of the *country*. Toronto's the capital of the province. If you look, there's probably a really big star beside Ottawa and a smaller one beside Toronto.

ALTHEA: Oh … you're right, I see that. Yes. Okay then.

Beat.

ALTHEA: Say that name again.

Michael begins to speak.

ALTHEA: No. Don't.

The door buzzes open. A song begins, and moves them towards one another.

SONG: '*Shto Mi E Milo*' (Macedonian)

Shto mi e milo, milo i drago
    (How I'd love to live, have a shop)
Vo Struga grada, mamo, duk'an da imam
    (In the village of Struga)

Lele varaj mome, mome Kalino
    (Hurry, young Kalino)
Vo Struga grada mamo duk'an da imam
    (In the village of Struga)

Silence. They stand together quite awkwardly in her front room. She's looking at him intensely. He has his notebook open in hand.

ALTHEA: You don't look Jewish.

MICHAEL: Really? Okay. Well, um, people say I look Armenian sometimes.

ALTHEA: Uh-huh.

MICHAEL: You know, the dark hair and the blue eyes.

ALTHEA: I don't know any Armenians. Is that what they look like?

MICHAEL: Some of them.

ALTHEA: Maybe the Jewish ones.

MICHAEL: (*to us*) She was in her sixties. Greying hair. Pale blue eyes, sad eyes, like a bloodhound's, like a … the sad, sick eyes of a … (*to her*) That was nice music you were listening to. Where was it from?

ALTHEA: What kind of writer?

MICHAEL: Sorry?

ALTHEA: You said you were a writer. What kind?

MICHAEL: Oh, ah …well, not really a – fiction, I guess. I won't write about you if that's –

ALTHEA: What do I have to do with your business in Poland?

MICHAEL: Oh, uh, nothing. But this, this man thought it might be good for me to talk to you.

ALTHEA: It would be good for *you*.

MICHAEL: And, he seemed to think, you know, you'd enjoy talking to someone.

ALTHEA: Enjoy?

MICHAEL: Well, yeah. He didn't actually use that word.

ALTHEA: What else did he say?

MICHAEL: Just that you'd worked together once. And that, um, your project didn't work out or something like that.

ALTHEA: Our project.

MICHAEL: Yeah. So! Mathias Todd. What kind of name is that? Is it German?

ALTHEA: Do you think it is?

MICHAEL: Don't you know?

Althea is silent.

MICHAEL: Okay.

ALTHEA: Nobody knows me here. Not in this country. And it's going to stay that way.

MICHAEL: … All right.

ALTHEA: This is all you need to know: I come from a country that used to be two.

MICHAEL: I'm sorry – I'm not sure I – ?

ALTHEA: Two neighbouring countries. But after World War II, the League of Nations redrew our borders, and we were annexed to our neighbours. They were on the losing side of the war and we were their punishment.

MICHAEL: (*trying to follow*) So, these were reparations?

ALTHEA: Did I say that?

MICHAEL: No, but – okay. Which country is this?

ALTHEA: I haven't told you that either, have I? Think of it this way: we were a mouse that the West put into a cat's cage. For the sake of the mouse, they said. There were a great many people murdered after that. And Mathias Todd was the cause of it. The one who made it happen. When it was all over, there was a commission struck to bring people to justice and I took a job with it as a prison guard. They chose me to watch over Todd. It was an honour. (*Beat.*)

MICHAEL: A prison guard. Huh … He was a politician, this Todd?

ALTHEA: You would probably call him an 'intellectual.' He was a professor at one of the main universities. He had 'ideas.'

MICHAEL: Ideas.

ALTHEA: 'Protect our traditions. Safeguard our children's future.' You know, harmless ideas. (*She sees he's writing.*) They killed two hundred thousand of us.

MICHAEL: What?

ALTHEA: Put that away.

MICHAEL: Oh … I'm just trying to keep track –

ALTHEA: For who? (*He doesn't answer.*) You will not write about me.

MICHAEL: No, no, of course not.

ALTHEA: (*Beat.*) Can I trust you?

Michael laughs.

ALTHEA: What?

MICHAEL: Nothing. I never used to get asked that question.

ALTHEA: Why do you get asked it now.

MICHAEL: Well, I recently had, I was put through a, a divorce, and –

ALTHEA: Never mind.

MICHAEL: (*Beat.*) I found out she was cheating on me.

ALTHEA: (*Beat.*) How.

MICHAEL: I ... read her ... I read her diary.

She stares at him.

ALTHEA: What did you say to this man, that he sent you to me?

MICHAEL: ... I'm not sure.

ALTHEA: And where was this bar?

MICHAEL: Um ... it's just across from you. Just down there.

SONG: '*Halala Kina*' (a Zimbabwean call-and-response song – sung quietly)

Halala Kina	(There is confusion)
Kina kimuhelele	(There a solution)

She crosses to her window and looks down.

ALTHEA: But he told you to come.

MICHAEL: He said you have something of his.

Mona	(Search)
Mona ko halleluya	(Search above for the answer)

ALTHEA: I see.

Kina / Kina kimuhelele
Mona / Mona ko halleluya

Althea smiles at some inner thought, turns from the window back to Michael. She has made a decision to tell Michael her story.

ALTHEA: Where was I? (*She looks at Michael, who doesn't seem to understand what she's saying.*) Where were we?

MICHAEL: (*He returns to his notebook, ready to write.*) Two hundred thousand?

ALTHEA: Mathias Todd fled the country after the killings. Went to Switzerland.

MICHAEL: So, this is Europe then.

ALTHEA: (*She looks at him.*) Put your little notebook away. (*Beat.*) It took us over ten years to get him back.

Lights come up behind them on the understairs of a municipal courthouse. Michael registers the presence of this world – an unexpected transformation has occurred. There is a cell with a prisoner in it, Mathias Todd. The younger Althea is present, watching. Todd looks haggard and older than his sixty years.

TODD: (*to Michael, quietly, with clarity*) Hello.

ALTHEA: When they brought him to the courthouse, he was sick. They claimed he was sick. Alzheimer's, his lawyers said. So he was put in the cells while they figured out what to do with him.

A buzzer goes in the background, and Young Althea delivers a tray of food to Todd. She puts it on a ledge on the side of the cage and pushes it through. Todd looks at it, and at her.

ALTHEA: Every day, I put food in front of him, but he wouldn't eat.

YOUNG ALTHEA: Starve, then.

ALTHEA: I'd leave the food on the ledge and we would both stare at it.

YOUNG ALTHEA: You forget how to eat?

Silence. After a moment, she goes to unlock the cage, bringing her chair along.

ALTHEA: But if he got sicker, if he starved, if he died, he would not stand trial, would he?

Young Althea enters the cage. By now, both the older Althea and Michael have turned to look at the scene from the past.

MICHAEL: So you fed him.

ALTHEA: It was my duty.

MICHAEL: I think that was the right thing to do.

ALTHEA: So we're in agreement.

We watch the younger Althea spoon feeding Todd. When the food enters his mouth, he eats helplessly, with profound hunger.

TODD: Oh. Thank you, Margaret.

YOUNG ALTHEA: I'm not Margaret.

TODD: This is very good, Margaret.

He holds his mouth open; she holds the spoon too far away.

ALTHEA: (*watching herself*) I had to feed him with a spoon, so he couldn't harm himself.

The young Althea jams the spoon into Todd's mouth, gagging him, but he does not register this as aggression, just copes with the discomfort.

YOUNG ALTHEA: What's wrong?

TODD: My mouth hurts.

YOUNG ALTHEA: You feel pain?

TODD: A little. What happened?

YOUNG ALTHEA: Your people shot my nephew in the mouth.

TODD: Afterwards, we should take a turn around the lake. I will catch you a frog!

Young Althea drops the tray at his feet with a clatter, stands and leaves the cell.

TODD: Where's my supper, Margaret?

YOUNG ALTHEA: That'll keep you alive until morning.

ALTHEA: His lawyers said, even if he was guilty, how could he stand trial if he was that sick?

MICHAEL: Erich Honecker had liver cancer.

ALTHEA: I beg your pardon?

MICHAEL: When they came to put Erich Honecker on trial, he was already dying. They had a hard time deciding if they had the moral right to try him.

ALTHEA: This has nothing to do with that.

MICHAEL: But you had a moral dilemma, too.

ALTHEA: No. We didn't.

MICHAEL: You say Mathias Todd was sick.

ALTHEA: I said they claimed he was sick.

MICHAEL: So he wasn't.

ALTHEA: Would you like me to write this all down on the back of an envelope and then you can call me later if you have any questions?

MICHAEL: I'd just like to be completely clear about what it is you're telling me.

ALTHEA: Let's just say the situation was ambiguous. You do know what 'ambiguous' means?

MICHAEL: Fine. Go on, then. You had your war criminal.

ALTHEA: Right. Although a charge of war crimes was too great a risk.

MICHAEL: You didn't have enough proof?

ALTHEA: We had proof. But we didn't want to lose him to a bunch of bureaucrats in the Hague. So he was charged with a single murder – not war crimes. We wanted this trial at home.

MICHAEL: He committed a murder that *wasn't* a war crime? He was busy.

ALTHEA: He killed a woman. Someone from my background.

MICHAEL: How was it not a war crime then? I thought he 'murdered' two hundred thousand of you.

ALTHEA: It was someone he had an affair with. This was before the purges.

MICHAEL: An affair? So he hated your – *kind* – but he fell in love with one?

ALTHEA: My kind?

MICHAEL: I mean –

ALTHEA: Stop. It's sweet that you think it was love. Who knows – maybe you're right. (*A quiet drone is added.*) But if it was, he corrected that flaw in himself.

SONG: '*A Salaam*' (from the Taaisha, a nomadic Islamic people from Central West Africa)

MIDDLE VOICES (MALE): *Yu Ma Hoy*
MIDDLE VOICES (FEMALE): *Bint al Haj / Shuffil Kho / Darinzan*
HIGH VOICE (FEMALE): *A Salaam*

(*This song, sung under the following, calls to the Mother – Ma – meaning all that comforts and provides. It then asks the daughter of the Haj to look for those in need, and to help them. 'Salaam' means 'Peace.'*)

TODD: (*to Michael*) What is this place we live in now? Is it 'ours' – is it 'theirs'? Once we had neighbours, and how nice it was! But when they suddenly found themselves annexed to this country, they must have thought, Where is our home? (*The women's voices join in.*) And we thought: why should they have been forced to live our way of life? Why should we live theirs? Ah, but when the Leaders of the Free World speak, we must listen! They have come to FIX us. They disturb the peace, (*One of the women's voices jumps up an octave.*) they broker a new peace, they send in their peacekeepers to keep the peace. And now that they have been and gone: chaos. That is their legacy. But where do those who nourish this chaos think it will lead us? (*The music finishes.*)

MICHAEL: (*to us*) It was a tape of a speech, with music in the background. It sounded familiar, but my memory for music – you can ask my ... ex. I think the only song I could ever remember the name of was 'Rundown Sally' –

JULIA: 'Runaround Sue.'

MICHAEL: Yeah, whatever. But the music sounded Arabic.

JULIA: Or maybe Hebrew?

MICHAEL: Uh – no. They were singing 'salaam,' not 'shalom.'

TODD: You sure it wasn't German? (*a laugh*) Maybe Armenian?

STEPHEN: Or Polish?

ALTHEA: It's not about music. It was a speech. A code. He gave
them a message. And they understood.

MICHAEL: What? Who did?

ALTHEA. *They* did.

TODD: Kill the others.

ALTHEA: He was their leader.

TODD: (*to Michael*) I'm sick.

Michael gets up and walks into the past to get closer to the story.

MICHAEL: Are you? (*to Althea*) Was he?

ALTHEA: He could remember things that had happened a long
time ago. And a few moments ago. But nothing in between.
Nothing that we wanted.

TODD: (*to Michael*) Look at my wedding ring.

He holds his ringless hand up to Michael.

ALTHEA: He had one story that drove me crazy.

TODD: Bedouin market. Twenty-four karat gold. Real rubies. Do you know where I bought this ring?

YOUNG ALTHEA: Be quiet!

TODD: I bought it in a Bedouin market, one for Margaret, one for me –

Young Althea comes and rips Todd's hand away from his face.

YOUNG ALTHEA: You're not wearing a ring!

TODD: Margaret? What's wrong?

YOUNG ALTHEA: (*pulling his hand up to show him*) Look.

TODD: Ahh. (*studying his hand*) Do you remember where I bought this ring?

YOUNG ALTHEA: Christ!

ALTHEA: When the disease progresses, it is as if a sheet of paper with your life written on it has begun burning right in the middle. You are a baby at the top of the page and it is today at the bottom, and the flame is slowly eating everything in between –

TODD: Real rubies.

Stephen, the state prosecutor, a man in his late thirties, comes in, applauding.

STEPHEN: Well done, Mathias. Alzheimer's! Good choice.

ALTHEA: They delayed the beginning of the trial.

STEPHEN: Good morning.

YOUNG ALTHEA: Good morning, sir. How are you?

STEPHEN: Excellent.

Julia, Todd's daughter, comes down the stairs behind. She is in her early thirties.

JULIA: I don't think you're supposed to be down here.

STEPHEN: I think I can go wherever I like.

MICHAEL: (*of Julia*) Who's this?

Althea, now drawn into the story she's telling, comes to join Michael in the past.

ALTHEA: That's Todd's daughter.

MICHAEL: (*a reverie*) Look at her.

STEPHEN: Yeah, I know.

MICHAEL: What's her name? (*Althea is about to answer*) Wait …
   Julia.

TODD: Margaret.

JULIA: Mum's not here right now, Dad. But I am. Julia.

TODD: Yes.

JULIA: You're in the courthouse, but I'm going to take you home
   soon.

STEPHEN: Oh, this is priceless.

ALTHEA: And that's Stephen Part. The lead prosecutor. A
   national hero.

STEPHEN: I was better looking than this.

ALTHEA: He brought Todd in.

She turns to look at Stephen and Julia, and they take this as a cue.

JULIA: (*to Stephen*) Do you really think my father would fake an illness rather than take the opportunity to clear his name?

STEPHEN: Miss Todd, if I were responsible for the deaths of five hundred thousand people, I'd fake an illness, too.

JULIA: That's NOT what he's charged with, Mr. Part, and you know it.

STEPHEN: This country will understand what it means to find him guilty here, Miss Todd. Even for one murder.

JULIA: How do I get you to understand the problem with your whole approach?

STEPHEN: Oh, I don't know – make me one of you?

MICHAEL: (*interrupting*) Sorry: 'five hundred thousand'? I thought it was two.

STEPHEN: It was five.

TODD: Do you know where I bought this ring?

STEPHEN: In a Bedouin market, in Syria, in 1960.

TODD: The man wanted 2000 dinar! I said to him, 'That is not twenty-four karat gold, those are not real rubies. I will not pay more than 500 dinar.'

JULIA: I know, Dad. Real rubies.

TODD: Ha! Your mother always said this ring was *gaudy*, Jules. It's not gaudy.

JULIA: (*delighted to hear her name*) No, Dad. It's beautiful!

STEPHEN: (*not surprised*) He just said your name.

JULIA: He knows who I am!

STEPHEN: You have to be careful, Mathias.

TODD: She loves me.

STEPHEN: (*to Althea*) Guard, call up and see if they're ready for us.

Althea goes nearly offstage to call upstairs.

JULIA: You're not supposed to be down here without our lawyer present.

STEPHEN: So, go get your lawyer. Take a look at this, Mathias.

Stephen takes out a coroner's report and holds it up against the bars.

JULIA: (*to Young Althea*) Excuse me?

TODD: Ah, Margaret!

STEPHEN: No, no, try again.

JULIA: Can you come back here, please?

TODD: Julia?

STEPHEN: Helena Sonnen! Is this Helena Sonnen, Mathias? (*suddenly yelling*) Surely you remember her!

TODD: (*Beat.*) Helena.

A low drone begins, accompanied by the distant voice of a woman singing – Todd is remembering Helena.

STEPHEN: Yes.

JULIA: He's only repeating you.

STEPHEN: No, we're having a conversation, Miss Todd. (*continuing, to Mathias*) Tell your daughter what you did with – I mean *to* – Helena Sonnen, Mathias.

Michael takes the report from Stephen and looks at it.

MICHAEL: So, this is the woman.

ALTHEA: This is the woman he killed.

MICHAEL: (*partly to himself*) She probably betrayed him.

The drone ends abruptly. Suddenly the characters all back off, like an image fading. Althea is watching Michael's reaction.

MICHAEL: What?

ALTHEA: Did I say that?

MICHAEL: No, no. I'm sorry – please keep going.

ALTHEA: Why don't you take some notes.

MICHAEL: Can I?

ALTHEA: Put this down. (*He opens the book.*) Mathias Todd was married to Margaret. His neighbour was named Helena.

MICHAEL: The woman he had the affair with. Helena Sonnen. Right. And she was of your, uh –

ALTHEA: 'Kind'? Yes, Michael. But Mathias got her pregnant. Her uncles found out and decided to teach him a lesson. So they killed his wife.

MICHAEL: Uh – What?

ALTHEA: First they forced him to confess his infidelity to Margaret, then they shot her in the head, in front of him. After that, Mathias walked over to Helena's and ran her through with a haying fork.

MICHAEL: Jesus. But she was –

ALTHEA: Pregnant with his child.

STEPHEN: Two lives on its points.

JULIA: He was innocent.

TODD: Write down that I was never convicted of anything.

ALTHEA: He had friends.

MICHAEL: (*to Todd*) How could you have done that?

TODD: Exactly! Horrible. She lived next door with her family, the poor thing. I saw them from time to time. We got along. (*to Althea*) I didn't even know she was pregnant.

ALTHEA: Her body was exhumed after he left the country. They ran the child's DNA. (*directed at Todd*) It was his.

TODD: Cut out the disease.

Michael begins to slip the report into his notebook.

JULIA: Give me that. Give me that!

Julia rips the report out of Michael's hand and tears it to shreds. But Stephen is holding an identical report as he did before, up against the bars.

STEPHEN: Speared them like animals. Is that how you remember it, Mathias? No sacrifice too great for the cause.

JULIA: This is a lie. (*She seizes the report from Stephen and tears it up.*)

STEPHEN: That's evidence!

JULIA: Evidence for your little inquisition.

STEPHEN: Something happened in this place, Miss Todd. Or do you have Alzheimer's too?

JULIA: How many people did your family lose? Tell me. TELL ME.

STEPHEN: I don't keep score the way you people do.

JULIA: I know how many. None. Your family had money and connections, unlike the poor countrymen you so identify with. Your people simply left, then you came back to go to law school, on scholarship, while I was in exile. The purges were the best thing that ever happened to you!

STEPHEN: Spoken like a true Todd. Maybe you'll inherit the family business.

JULIA: THE PURGES WERE NOT MY FATHER'S FAULT. (*Pause.*) You must be the only person in the whole world who thinks what happened in this country was caused by one person's *thoughts*.

MICHAEL: Well, that *is* a good point.

JULIA: Thank you.

MICHAEL: I'm just saying.

ALTHEA: You're just saying what?

MICHAEL: People should be held responsible for their actions, not their thoughts.

ALTHEA: And where do you think actions come from, Michael?

Young Althea returns.

YOUNG ALTHEA: They just called down, sir.

STEPHEN: Excellent. (*He begins to leave.*)

YOUNG ALTHEA: Sir.

Stephen is stopped by her tone.

They're still in chambers.

STEPHEN: (*surprised by this*) What? Really. Well, they can't be much longer. (*to Julia*) See you upstairs.

JULIA: On our way out.

STEPHEN: Right.

He begins to leave, thinks of something else.

STEPHEN: You know, you won't defend him once you've heard all the evidence.

JULIA: He doesn't need to be defended.

STEPHEN: (*quietly to her*) You think no one's tried this before? I've put eight years into this case. But when the people upstairs finally declare him fit to stand, his little act down here will convict him better than anything I can say.

JULIA: How are you going to feel when you realize you've been torturing a sick man?

STEPHEN: It doesn't worry me.

JULIA: The only thing my father ever did was make a private mistake.

STEPHEN: A private mistake?

JULIA: His *affair*. That's the only thing he's guilty of. The only thing he ever hid from us, from anyone.

STEPHEN: (*Musing – no longer really talking to her, he's constructing something he can use against them.*) The only thing he ever hid from us. (*Beat.*) He lied to you. He lied then, he lies now. He's a liar. Isn't he? Thank you, Miss Todd. See you upstairs.

He leaves. After a beat:

JULIA: Shit. Wait! Hold on a second!

She follows him out.

TODD: Margaret?

MICHAEL: And?

TODD: Margaret?

MICHAEL: What happened next?

ALTHEA: They went upstairs. I have no idea what was said after that.

MICHAEL: But I want to know about her.

ALTHEA: Obviously.

TODD: MARGARET!

MICHAEL: BE QUIET! God, you must have wanted to kill him.

ALTHEA: (*Beat.*) I tried not to pay any attention to him.

YOUNG ALTHEA: (*Suddenly turns on her older self.*) *Please.* You were like mother and child. Whenever you were alone with him, it was like he belonged to you. Him and whatever was inside of him, all yours.

ALTHEA: You wanted to destroy him.

YOUNG ALTHEA: No. No, I didn't. I wanted justice. For my dead. Didn't I?

ALTHEA: Yes. Of course you did. (*to Michael, covering an emotion that has suddenly welled up*) I was a lovely young woman. You would have liked me. Will you have a soda?

MICHAEL: No, it's –

She goes off anyway. Todd and Michael are alone onstage.

MICHAEL: What the hell is – ? (*to the audience, waving notebook*) I'm sorry, this thing isn't coming together. I feel like I'm painting a room and the old wallpaper keeps leaking through. I don't even know if I'm describing this right. You have to imagine this apartment. (*He gets up to demonstrate the things he saw.*) There were curtains here, over the two windows, so it was dark even though it was the middle of the day. Dark. Airless. Claustrophobic. You can see this, right? I'm trying to describe … Althea. I don't want to make her look like she was unkind to me. I mean, she was the only person I met on that side of the ocean who was willing to talk! About anything. Although she *was* lonely. Her loneliness was all over the place, like a stain on everything.

TODD: Why don't you shut up? (*He has Michael's attention.*) You talk a lot, but you don't say anything.

MICHAEL: At least I remember what I've done.

TODD: Do you?

MICHAEL: Yes.

TODD: What do you think of this: all the evil in the world is due to love. An excess of love.

MICHAEL: If you love too much you hate? That's your big conclusion about human nature.

TODD: When I killed Helena Sonnen, I came.

MICHAEL: You'll do it again when they hang you. (*calling off*) Althea, can we – ?

TODD: You loved your wife.

MICHAEL: Of course I did.

TODD: (*with mock empathy*) But now you hate her.

MICHAEL: I don't hate anyone.

TODD: How did you feel reading her diary? That was nice, wasn't it? Being inside her, inside her *head*. Listening to her private thoughts. Think of owning something like that. When I spoke to the stupid, terrified people of my country, it was as if my tongue slithered into their skulls and spat 'murder.' I think you'd like that power.

MICHAEL: (*off, getting worried*) Althea?

TODD: Where do those who nourish this chaos think it will lead?

Althea re-enters, hands Michael a very small glass of water.

ALTHEA: I don't have any soda.

MICHAEL: Oh, that's –

ALTHEA: I wanted justice. For my dead.

MICHAEL: (*taken aback*) Okay …

Young Althea walks past Todd's cell.

TODD: Margaret?

YOUNG ALTHEA: Do I look like your wife?

MICHAEL: Did you look like her?

ALTHEA: We were almost the same age. About the age Margaret was when she was killed. He mixed us up.

MICHAEL: You were alone with him a lot.

ALTHEA: I lived down there.

TODD: Margaret?

Young Althea looks at him.

TODD: Margaret?

YOUNG ALTHEA: (*angry*) What is it? (*Beat. Then, seeing her opportunity, says softly*) What is it, dear?

TODD: Have we eaten?

YOUNG ALTHEA: No. No, not yet. Did you … did you happen see the paper this morning?

TODD: Bring it in if you're done with it, love.

YOUNG ALTHEA: They say they caught that man they were looking for. That professor … what was his name?

TODD: It must be lunchtime.

YOUNG ALTHEA: Are you listening to me?

TODD: Sorry, Margaret. A professor?

YOUNG ALTHEA: Yes! They captured him. Do you know what he did?

TODD: Yes.

YOUNG ALTHEA: Do you?

TODD: (*delighted*) I shall have a coddled egg for lunch!

YOUNG ALTHEA: Listen to me. He, his men, *put a gun* in the mouth of a little boy and shot him in front of his parents and his aunt!

TODD: No, no.

YOUNG ALTHEA: How could that happen? How could a man do that?

TODD: (*A beat. He seems to be considering her.*) He should die.

YOUNG ALTHEA: Who should?

TODD: (*He looks at his ring.*) Will you look at this? Do you know where I got this ri–

YOUNG ALTHEA: You are a murderer. Do you understand? A murderer … (*struggling for control*) They're going to figure you out, they're going to open you up and find you wherever you are in there, and then you will say, to all of us, to the world, 'I am Mathias Ernesti Todd, I am the BUTCHER, I sit at the right hand of DEATH!!'

Young Althea thrusts her arms into the cell, as if to strangle Todd. He grasps her arms, but instead of defending himself, he comforts her.

TODD: Now, now … be calm. There is nothing to be done.

She lets herself be held by him.

YOUNG ALTHEA: I want you to die.

TODD: … nothing to be done …

YOUNG ALTHEA: I know.

Todd begins to sing tenderly to her, a folk song.

SONG: '*Zasp'o Janko*' (Croatian)

> *Zasp'o Janko pod jablanom*
>> (Zaspo slept beneath a poplar tree)

Svoje mile drage
>(Belonging to his sweetheart)

Young Althea and Todd will slowly begin to dance. As they do, the song fills the space.

Refrain:
Lepe moje crne ovci,
>(My lovely dark eyes)
Pogledajte ne me.
>(Look up at me)

Pod jablanom zlatnom granom
>(Under the golden poplar branch)
Svoje mile drage
>(Belonging to his sweetheart)

Young Althea are now dancing.

ALTHEA: It was a strange relationship.

The dance continues. Althea stares at her younger self bound together with Todd.

ALTHEA: You would never have been able to tell the difference between our peoples. We looked the same, our religions were practically identical, we spoke the same language. Why was there hate between us? (*Beat.*) Because *their* bread was raised and ours was *fermented*? Because our songs sounded like theirs, but with different words?

MICHAEL: It must have been more than that.

ALTHEA: Why? Maybe there was something in themselves that they hated, and they saw it in us.

MICHAEL: Familiarity breeding.

ALTHEA: Yes. 'Salaam' and 'Shalom.'

MICHAEL: Well, no. There are plenty of differences between Arabs and Jews.

ALTHEA: To you.

SONG: '*Di Saposhkelech*' (Jewish)

Julia appears, humming an old Jewish song about a man who would sacrifice anything for his love: 'I'd sell my boots, and ride in open carriages, just to be with you …'

As Althea speaks, Julia goes into the cell to visit with her father.

ALTHEA: Todd was everywhere in those days. The university gave him fame. He spoke on everything that happened in the country. Tradition and pride. He spoke of peace, but we heard him say, 'Hide or we'll find you and kill you,' and they heard him say, 'Find them and kill them.'

JULIA: No, Dad, it's Julia.

MICHAEL: I don't know what to think of her. She was all I had.

ALTHEA: What?

MICHAEL: Sorry, you were saying about Julia –

JULIA: Your daughter. You're at the courthouse. They're going to let us go soon.

TODD: Yes.

ALTHEA: She was very loving with him. A good daughter.

TODD: Where's Margaret?

YOUNG ALTHEA: It's five o'clock. You need to go soon.

JULIA: I want to shave him.

YOUNG ALTHEA: A nurse will do it when it's necessary.

JULIA: I don't want a nurse to do it. If you were in my shoes, would you allow a stranger in here with a razor?

YOUNG ALTHEA: That's why you're not coming in here with one. And I'm not in your shoes.

JULIA: Your people have blood on their hands as well.

YOUNG ALTHEA: We fought back.

JULIA: Is that what you call it? (*She comes out of the cell.*) I want a guarantee that Mr. Part is never left alone with my father.

YOUNG ALTHEA: You can trust us, Miss Todd, to ensure your father is safe and secure at all times. You have nothing to fear.

JULIA: (*Pause. Chooses not to respond.*) In the morning, when I come for his breakfast, I'm going to bring a razor. I'll hide it in my bag if you like.

YOUNG ALTHEA: A safety razor.

JULIA: I'll need some hot water and some towels as well.

She begins to leave.

JULIA: Let's remember the laws of this country still have a presumption of innocence.

YOUNG ALTHEA: Which laws are you talking about? The ones that you people wrote? Because I don't recall that presumption being granted to anyone *I* knew.

Julia cannot reply.

YOUNG ALTHEA: (*moving away from Julia*) I'll let you in early, tomorrow.

TODD: (*calling to Young Althea as she passes*) Margaret?

JULIA: (*to Young Althea*) I know you have goodness in you. I can feel it.

YOUNG ALTHEA: (*calling back, hard*) You have two minutes, Miss Todd.

Young Althea walks away from Julia.

TODD: (*suddenly confused, agitated – looking now to Julia*) Margaret, Margaret?

JULIA: No, Dad. Dad. Margaret is not here. (*She tries to calm her father.*) Listen. Listen. (*He comes to stillness.*) You know she's dead.

TODD: Margaret.

JULIA: Yes, Margaret. They murdered her. Your wife. My mother.

TODD: My mother.

JULIA: NO, DAD. Listen to what I'm saying. My mother was Margaret. Margaret was your wife. I'm your daughter. Margaret and Mathias's daughter. Julia.

TODD: (*irritated*) I know. I know who you are.

JULIA: Do you know that you're sick?

TODD: I'm not sick. I just don't ... I can't remember. Everything.

JULIA: You *are* sick, Dad. (*searching his eyes, then quietly*) Right?

TODD: What?

JULIA: (*quietly*) You wouldn't lie to me. Would you?

TODD: (*Beat.*) Where are we?

JULIA: The courthouse.

TODD: Take me inside. Where is your mother?

JULIA: Dad ...

TODD: There's nothing wrong with me!

YOUNG ALTHEA: (*returning*) I heard that.

JULIA: He just asked for my mother, and she's been dead for more than twenty years.

YOUNG ALTHEA: He could be lying to you as well, Miss Todd.

JULIA: (*considering him*) He isn't. I know he isn't.

She touches his face. He grasps her violently.

TODD: BLOODY PEOPLE!

JULIA: Ow! Dad – let go of –

TODD: Swarming our ... the places we built!

Todd throws Julia to the ground.

MICHAEL: Jesus ... what happened?

ALTHEA: *Listen.*

JULIA: Althea! Unlock the door!

YOUNG ALTHEA: Listen to what he's saying.

JULIA: Althea! Unlock this door!

Young Althea remains motionless, watching.

MICHAEL: (*to Althea*) And you just watched?

TODD: (*grasping his daughter's throat*) Get the fuck off my lake!

Young Althea remains inactive, watching.

ALTHEA: I stopped him. (*on Michael's look*) I did.

Todd is now strangling Julia. Young Althea waits a moment longer to see if this is a ploy, but then becomes convinced that Todd really is going to kill Julia and leaps into the struggle. She unlocks the door to pull Julia out, but Todd's strength is immense.

TODD: Filthy woman!

YOUNG ALTHEA: It's Margaret, Mathias! It's Julia! Let go of her!

TODD: Do you hear what she says about me? I would never touch you! You filthy –

JULIA: Please Dad –

TODD: (*confused and desolate*) LOVE?! Never!

Young Althea begins to beat Todd, and he finally releases Julia, who falls back into her arms.

MICHAEL: My god. Was she hurt?

ALTHEA: She lived.

MICHAEL: He could have killed her.

ALTHEA: Anything could have happened.

The two women stand back from the cell, where Todd now paces like a trapped tiger. Julia is trying to catch her breath.

YOUNG ALTHEA: Do you want me to call a doctor.

JULIA: No, don't …

ALTHEA: He didn't know what he was doing.

YOUNG ALTHEA: He doesn't know what he's doing.

JULIA: (*Julia refocuses her attention on Young Althea.*) Do you really mean that?

YOUNG ALTHEA: I'm not your friend, Miss Todd.

JULIA: But you must know by now …

YOUNG ALTHEA: I do. (*Silence.*) I want to reach him. And I've tried. I've slept down here, next to the cell, listening … but he talks … nonsense.

JULIA: Then tell the court that.

YOUNG ALTHEA: It's not my place to tell the court anything.

JULIA: But they'll listen to you. (*Young Althea just stares at her.*) Please. Look. I have my doubts, too.

YOUNG ALTHEA: No you don't –

JULIA: About what happened in this country. He sent me away after my mother was killed. I don't know if he … I don't know.

YOUNG ALTHEA: You don't know if he what?

JULIA: I lived far away from here.

YOUNG ALTHEA: You don't care what happened.

JULIA: I do, but it's not the point any more. You can't put a man on trial who forgets three decades of his life! He can't even deny what he's accused of.

YOUNG ALTHEA: His illness is the denial.

JULIA: You and I have the same purpose, and –

YOUNG ALTHEA: (*rounding on her*) Don't you say that! Don't you dare say that!

JULIA: I mean, we both want justice.

YOUNG ALTHEA: No, we don't. You want someone to fix this for you. But what I want is beyond your power to give.

JULIA: (*Beat.*) You've given up.

YOUNG ALTHEA: You will as well. His disease is going to eat everyone's hope.

JULIA: Althea.

YOUNG ALTHEA: Don't use my first name.

JULIA: Help us.

YOUNG ALTHEA: You don't know my dead.

JULIA: (*Beat.*) You're right. I'm sorry.

She leaves, but Michael is watching intently, certain she won't leave it like this. But she doesn't return.

MICHAEL: 'You're right, I'm sorry'? (*to Althea*) That's what she said?

ALTHEA: She didn't press me any further.

MICHAEL: Well, you're not the easiest person to talk to, are you? (*to Julia*) She just told you she knows your father is sick. You don't give up now.

JULIA: You heard her. I don't know her dead.

MICHAEL: That has nothing to do with the present situation!

ALTHEA: You take her side.

MICHAEL: I don't. I just don't understand how she could have walked away from you.

ALTHEA: I should never have told you she was beautiful.

MICHAEL: She was *savvy.* (*Beat.*) There's more here. Remember when she followed Stephen out of the room? You said you didn't know what happened next.

Michael moves Stephen into the scene.

STEPHEN: He lied then, he lies now. He's a liar. Isn't he? Thank you, Miss Todd. See you upstairs.

Michael moves Julia into the scene.

JULIA: Shit. Wait! Hold on a second!

Michael watches the next scene unfold. He is now writing the dialogue between Julia and Stephen. Their acting changes slightly as a result.

JULIA: Stephen.

STEPHEN: What?

JULIA: It doesn't have to be like this, with the two of us at each other's throats.

ALTHEA: *Excuse me.*

MICHAEL: Just let me finish –

JULIA: You want a trial and I want my father. Tell your people *we are not like them, we are* –

MICHAEL: *merciful* –

JULIA: (*overlapping*) – *merciful* and let my father return to Geneva.

ALTHEA: What are you doing?

MICHAEL: I'm working this out.

JULIA: And after you let him go, you arrest me – The Daughter. Charged with sheltering a suspected war criminal. And you have your trial.

ALTHEA: For god's sake.

MICHAEL: Don't you think she would have tried this?

ALTHEA: It doesn't matter what she tried. This is all in the past. Speculating on something I never saw or heard is pointless.

MICHAEL: Aren't you curious, though? About what she was thinking?

ALTHEA: Why don't you just come out and say it:

Althea regains control of the dialogue, and uses it to mock Michael's imagined version of events. The acting expands again.

JULIA: I already carry the 'burden' of being a Todd. I can bear it for him, too.

MICHAEL: Well, don't simplify.

ALTHEA: No. This *is* where you're going. Listen!

JULIA: I'm not afraid to pay the cost of his freedom.

STEPHEN: Your courage startles and moves me, Miss Todd. Are you really this brave? (*to Michael*) She could get to me, I totally buy it.

ALTHEA: And then they fall in love and nothing ever goes wrong for anybody ever again.

MICHAEL: Don't make me out to be an idiot just because I'm interested in what was going through her mind.

ALTHEA: Too bad I don't have her diary for you.

MICHAEL: Not nice.

ALTHEA: I'm telling you everything I know. Why do you want more?

MICHAEL: Why aren't you more curious?

ALTHEA: You had a divorce.

MICHAEL: That has nothing to do with this.

ALTHEA: Exactly. But you can't figure out what went wrong with your own story, so you're going to straighten out mine.

MICHAEL: That's not what I was –

JULIA: You don't get to reinvent your world using me.

YOUNG ALTHEA: Using us.

STEPHEN: User.

MICHAEL: I just thought it would be interesting to consider that she might have been willing to *sacrifice* her–

ALTHEA: Well then, she probably just ran out and offered to fuck Stephen in exchange for her father's freedom.

JULIA: How about it, big boy?

STEPHEN: Well ... hot diggity! (*calling to Young Althea*) Let the old guy go! C'mere you –

They kiss furiously.

MICHAEL: All right, enough. Why don't you just cut to the chase then, okay? Todd stood trial or he didn't. He went to jail, he hanged, he's living in a condo in Argentina. I have a plane to catch.

ALTHEA: So go catch it.

Stalemate.

ALTHEA: You think it's easy for me to tell you this story?

MICHAEL: I know it isn't.

ALTHEA: I don't care if you want a tidy, happy ending.

MICHAEL: I'm not interested in an easy –

ALTHEA: Good, because my story isn't 'easy.' The people in it don't behave courageously. They're selfish and they're blind – and your noble little woman there? She gets a bullet in the face.

Michael stares at her.

ALTHEA: Oh, so I have your attention now?

MICHAEL: What are you talking about?

YOUNG ALTHEA: (*of Julia*) She's dead.

ALTHEA: You want to tart that up a bit?

MICHAEL: (*to Julia*) You're dead?

JULIA: For more than twenty years, now.

MICHAEL: (*Beat.*) My god … why does everything keep –

ALTHEA: What – ?

MICHAEL: GOING TO HELL! GOING TO SHIT! I can't fucking stand it. I am *not* going to put myself through – This is not heading in any direction that interests me, okay? I'm sorry, I apologize, but I can't –

ALTHEA: You can't – ?

MICHAEL: I have things to do before my flight. And, frankly, all you seem to care about is making me look some some clueless fuckwit anyway.

JULIA: Prick. You got what you deserved.

MICHAEL: (*warning her*) You should watch what you –

ALTHEA: Sit. Down.

Silence.

MICHAEL: I came to you of my own free –

ALTHEA: No, you didn't. You were sent to me. Remember?

Michael looks at her.

But why you? Out of a barful of men and women, he could have talked to anyone. Why did he pick you?

Michael can't answer that.

MICHAEL: Please. Let me go now. Okay?

ALTHEA: Touch me. (*Beat.*) DO IT.

He begins to tentatively reach out to her. Althea grabs his hand and presses it to her face.

ALTHEA: Am I real?

MICHAEL: Yes.

ALTHEA: I live and breathe?

MICHAEL: Yes!

ALTHEA: Good.

The three women sing.

SONG: '*Vreme mi dojde*' (Bulgarian)

> *Vreme mi dojde, dzan'm Mavrode*
>> (High noon has come, Mavrode)
> *Vreme pladnino, je*
>> (There is no shade)

ALTHEA: You sit down. And listen to my story.

Helpless, he comes to the chair, but, before he takes his seat: blackout.

Act Two

We hear Althea's voice before we see her. She's singing. Lights come up on Althea, facing out at Stage Left, drinking from a mug of tea. As she speaks the following, the lights come up on Michael at Stage Right, listening to her. The rest of the stage is in darkness, although we sense presences there.

SONG: '*Tobela*' (Zimbabwean)

Iyo-o / Iyo-o / Iyo-o	(a soothing sound)
Ayitobela Murena	(O Pray to God)
Iyo-o / Iyo-o / Iyo-o	(a soothing sound)
Ayitobela Murena	(O Pray to God)

Chorus:
Tobela Murena / Tobela Murena
Tobela Murena / Tobela Murena

Horiyatsa	(Look around / pay attention)
Hamuzani waka	(To what is happening)
Tobela	(Pray)
Ayitobela Murena	(O Pray to God)

Chorus:
Tobela Murena / Tobela Murena
Tobela Murena / Tobela Murena

ALTHEA: Do you believe in your own death? Every moment you are alive is endless and the present goes on and on with you inside it. Of course the end is truly coming, but it's so far off, and, in the meantime, the spring bulbs need bringing out of the dark and the windows must be cleaned. These distant murmurings of unrest are like the way you sometimes hear your name on the wind and you shudder. Because it's *eerie* that the wind should know your name.

She hands Michael his tea.

But something is growing. Somewhere, always, people are unhappy. Rumours take on flesh, and then, as if in a fairy tale, we see the torches coming down our street. We must hide! Quickly, silently, tell the children not to say a word! How is it possible that this very morning I made bread with my sister, and now I wait with her in the dark? Outside, they've already begun to kill. We hear glass breaking and sudden shouts, followed by silence.

You're hiding now, standing behind your wife's dresses in your closet and they find you there and drag you out to the street, throw you down and the blood is roaring in your ears as you feel around in the dirt for your glasses and around you a human noose is tightening. You beg for your life, and in begging you've already given it. It's theirs, they realize this, it is an astonishing power. What was once unimaginable becomes simple and suddenly common. Like an instinct they didn't know they had. They kill with whatever is at hand. With stones and wooden clubs, with knives, with bullets, with their own hands and feet – ancient forms of murder – and you feel your body, this inviolate body that has been yours alone since the moment you entered the world, is being broken apart. You are going to die, *this* is your death. And then, seeing you dead, they look on you, breathless, and with wonder they think *imagine what that was, to have deserved this fate. (Pause.)*

How's your tea?

MICHAEL: My ... ? Fine.

ALTHEA: There's more.

MICHAEL: (*of the tea, confused*) More ... ?

Althea looks at him. She doesn't mean the tea.

MICHAEL: (*paralyzed*) Okay.

ALTHEA: They entered our houses. Came in as if they belonged there and we didn't. We looked at them with pity. We'd had them as dinner guests once and now they smashed the plates and broke the wineglasses. They put my parents into the back of a pickup truck and drove them off. We never saw them again.

MICHAEL: Were there camps?

ALTHEA: No. They spared themselves that expense. They took my parents to the edge of town and just shot them. Left the bodies uncovered in a field. I found my father's suit jacket on a skeleton five months later. His best suit. And then, after that, taking people away somewhere was too much trouble. They just came and killed. They found me and my sister and her husband, their little boy, and some friends of ours, and they made us go to a church. They pushed us up to the altar – where we read from so many of the same texts as they did in their own churches – and they made us perform. We had to sing our old national anthem. They told us to stand on one leg and said we were storks and said they were storks, too. Pointing their guns at us. If you put a leg down, they acted surprised and said that you were only *pretending* to be a stork and then they shot you. My nephew, Domenic, began laughing when my sister put her foot down. And they said to him, 'Why are you laughing?' and he said it was because, of all the things that could make you die, imagine that it would look like a schoolyard game. They took him out of the line and put the gun in his mouth and told him to laugh some more and they would spare him. And out of him came this unworldly laughter, as if the sun and the moon were laughing at the stupidity of being human. It was a real laugh, a deep, deep laugh. And they shot out the back of his head and he stopped.

A pause. Michael perhaps attempts to, but is unable to speak.

They killed us all. Except me. I was last and … they sent me home. I don't know why. (*Beat.*) Maybe so there would be one person left to tell of their might.

Althea begins to sing very quietly to herself.

SONG: '*Binaya*' (Taaisha, Central West Africa)

Binaya la bis stobu sala daneh bifoghu
Binaya mashi mashi hu sala daneh bifighu
Binaya Binaya Binaya Binaya

(This is a song sung by a grandmother to a child who is on the cusp of adolescence – a song of goodbye to a little one who is growing up.)

Long pause. We can hear them breathing.

MICHAEL: Would it be okay … if I had glass of plain water?

She gets up and leaves. He watches her, then turns again, puts his head in his hands. He's completely undone.

TODD: Hey. (*He gets Michael's attention.*) How's it going?

MICHAEL: I don't want to talk right now.

TODD: Are you questioning any of this? Does her story make her an expert in anything but her own suffering? I thought you knew something about that.

STEPHEN: You remember what your ex used to say, right, Mike?

JULIA: You just see what you want to see.

Michael takes the notebook away from Julia.

TODD: Of course she's going to make it sound like the slaughter of the innocents. 'Poor us, sitting there not doing anything to anyone.' Except *breeding*.

MICHAEL: (*of what's happening onstage, to us*) Sorry about this –

STEPHEN: (*to Todd*) Well, I believe her. She's speaking from the heart. You can't fake that.

JULIA: Of course you believe her. She justifies everything you're doing.

STEPHEN: No. No – It's important personal history.

TODD: There's no such thing. Not from the perspective of nations. Everything that happens to *people* disappears. They forget what they see – what they learn and do. They forget.

MICHAEL: Look! I'm trying to think here!

STEPHEN: Is that what you're doing?

TODD: I must admit I am getting a little bored. All I get to do is look confused and drool a little. (*He takes Michael's notebook.*) Now, *this* stuff is interesting. (*reading*) 'I remember J– saying she thought Colin was boring.'

JULIA: (*looking at the notebook*) What does the J stand for?

MICHAEL: (*taking his notebook back*) This is private!

JULIA: Oh, *your* life is private, is it?

STEPHEN: But he'll write about *this* –

TODD: He's not going to write about this. He promised.

A beat.

MICHAEL: You people are part of history. I don't owe you anything.

STEPHEN: We're not part of your history.

MICHAEL: You think genocide isn't part of my history?

JULIA: Not Althea's genocide.

MICHAEL: I can tell whatever story I want.

STEPHEN: Evidently.

Michael succeeds in tearing away the notebook. Holds it to himself.

MICHAEL: (*opening the notebook and flipping through*) No ... no, I'm not doing this. Okay? I'm here to talk about your father. And whatever he remembers or doesn't remember, people who agreed with his politics killed Althea's entire family. It doesn't matter if he didn't actually do anything, he certainly didn't try to stop it.

JULIA: How the hell do you know?

MICHAEL: Because it's more believable that he didn't! Your father either goaded a country of stupid farmers –

JULIA: (*to Stephen*) Stupid farmers?

MICHAEL: – into murdering thousands of people, or he sat back and enjoyed watching it! And there's someone just like him behind every haystack. One of them turned a gun on the inhabitants of a little town where my mother's people lived. *That's* why I have a right to tell this story! I would have had forty or fifty cousins if not for your father!

JULIA: It wasn't *my* father –

MICHAEL: It might as well have been! Why not?

JULIA: Because he would still have been in school at the time, and he didn't live in Poland.

MICHAEL: It's a metaphor. Okay? Someone *just like* your father!

STEPHEN: Isn't that a simile?

MICHAEL: Screw off. Christ, I'm arguing with imaginary people.

TODD: You keep telling yourself that.

JULIA: Maybe you just like blaming others for things you're too cowardly to do yourself.

MICHAEL: And maybe you're a lying cheating bitch who doesn't care who she hurts.

She stares at him, smiling faintly. Then goes off. He's alone. Althea brings Michael his water, and he drinks it all down.

ALTHEA: Feverishly taking notes, are you?

MICHAEL: It doesn't help.

ALTHEA: It's all right. I want you to.

MICHAEL: You want me to write it down.

ALTHEA: I thought about it. Who am I to say I own an atrocity? Go ahead.

He hesitates.

ALTHEA: Because you're going to anyway. Aren't you? (*No response from him.*) So do it in front of me. Do it. Open it up.

MICHAEL: (*to us*) It felt like the darkness of that little room was seeping into me. Whatever was inside of her, I didn't want it in this book, infecting my own thoughts. Infecting me. (*to Althea, standing*) I should –

ALTHEA: What's your hurry?

He's aware of the other characters watching him.

MICHAEL: Look, maybe can we go somewhere else? I can buy you a cup of coffee or a drink if you want.

ALTHEA: You don't like my apartment now?

MICHAEL: I find it a little dark in here.

ALTHEA: That's how I like it. (*Beat.*) Write it down. (*He doesn't move.*) Write it down. 'She liked to keep her rooms dark.'

She's not backing off, so he opens his book and starts writing.

ALTHEA: 'It was a small apartment. No art on the walls. Just a couch and a chair and a little throw rug.' (*He's still writing.*) 'The way she lived, it was like she couldn't bear to be reminded of all the life beyond her walls. The living pained her. Children hurt her eyes.' (*He's stopped writing.*) Am I getting too personal here now?

MICHAEL: (*closing the book*) Why don't we just get back to your story? Okay? You said Julia Todd died. Tell me how that happened.

ALTHEA: (*Beat.*) Someone killed her.

MICHAEL: Fine. Then how about the man in the bar. You know who he is.

ALTHEA: He's someone who left part of himself with me. Do you know what that's like?

Long beat as Michael waits for her, wills her, to go on. She doesn't.

MICHAEL: How did Julia die?

ALTHEA: I'm not ready to tell you that.

MICHAEL: Why did you take that job? As a guard?

YOUNG ALTHEA: To serve my country.

MICHAEL: Do you really think you served your country?

YOUNG ALTHEA: I must have. It still exists.

MICHAEL: That's not what I mean. Did you go in to do good, or just to get revenge?

YOUNG ALTHEA: I wanted. To serve. My country.

MICHAEL: The UN would have served your country – by trying Todd at the Hague. You're leaving something out.

ALTHEA: Am I?

YOUNG ALTHEA: The UN let the genocide run for ten years before they sent their peacekeepers in, after they figured we were all gone.

MICHAEL: The international courts would have known what to do with him.

YOUNG ALTHEA: We knew what to do with him.

MICHAEL: You knew what you *wanted* to do with him.

YOUNG ALTHEA: *We had him*. Here. In this place where he'd done so much evil. Wouldn't you have wanted that chance?

MICHAEL: With who?

YOUNG ALTHEA: Oh, gosh. Hitler? Mengele?

MICHAEL: We got our trials and we got as much justice as was possible.

YOUNG ALTHEA: But you didn't.

MICHAEL: First off, Hitler was dead. And the Holocaust happened all over Europe, not in one place. There was a *structure* to the system, and everyone followed it.

YOUNG ALTHEA: Exactly. You followed. You sat in the room and watched. That's what you understand – watching. But what if you'd had the chance we did? The man himself, standing in front of you, your eyes on his? You have no idea what it would have been like to get justice on your own terms.

MICHAEL: It shouldn't be *my* terms. Alone.

YOUNG ALTHEA: Really? Didn't you just visit Poland on a personal vendetta?

MICHAEL: Don't try that.

YOUNG ALTHEA: Ustrzyki Dolne, tak? There's a man there you never found a trace of, whose name you never discovered. But he existed, and you know he did. Let's call him Tomas Stanczyk.

SONG: '*Szerelem, szerelem*' (Hungarian)

A drone begins.

Todd stands.

YOUNG ALTHEA: He was a doctor. Deputized by the Einsatz-gruppen – someone the Nazis knew people would listen to. Well-liked. On the afternoon of October 12, 1941, he ordered his men to round up all the Jews in the town.

SONG: *Szerelem, szerelem* (Love, love)

They take them, tied together by the wrists, into the town square, where their neighbours have already gathered to watch.

SONG: *Átkozott gyötrelem* (Wretched suffering)

Doctor Stancyck raises his hand. There are three hundred Jews, including your great-grandparents and seven of their children. They've all been to him at one time or another. They trust him.

SONG: *Szerelem, szerelem*

They shoot them and they go down like stalks of wheat before the reaper. All this man does is lower his arm.

SONG: *Átkozott gyötrelem*

She puts a club, maybe a machete, in Michael's hand.

And here he is.

TODD: They fell as if trained to die. Standing in the light of a bright fall day, ravens in the trees watching everything, the people standing around, some coming home from the bakery with fresh bread on the backs of their bicycles.

MICHAEL: None of the people I met there claimed to remember anything.

TODD: You should have spoken to the ravens.

MICHAEL: And what happened to you?

TODD: I married happily – very happily – had five children, and died in my sleep at the age of seventy-nine, three years more than God allots. My wife still enjoys my pension.

Todd crosses to sit, then picks up and sips Michael's tea. Michael moves behind him with the machete.

In your bloodline alone, there are sixty fewer Jews in the world today than there would have been if we hadn't chopped at the roots when we did. It will take another hundred and thirty years for the population of the Jews in the world to reach pre-war numbers. And little kikes like you are still running around looking to justify their existence somehow.

Michael raises the machete. He is in stasis – unable to strike, unable to relax – staring at Todd.

All those people – real people – died for you, and the best you can manage is a little play?

Michael can take no more. He rushes at Todd with the machete, screaming. Young Althea catches his arm. Michael strains against her.

TODD: Rubies. Real rubies.

Young Althea disarms Michael, who stands staring at Mathias.

ALTHEA: (*to Michael*) How could you have done that?

MICHAEL: (*turning, defending himself to Althea*) I didn't do anything! He –

ALTHEA: He what?

The cast looks to Michael, waiting for his response.

MICHAEL: I was provoked.

YOUNG ALTHEA: Imagine that.

Julia enters with her shaving things and is let into the cell.

JULIA: Thank you.

YOUNG ALTHEA: Be quick about it.

JULIA: He's going to look so nice with a smooth face. You're going to be handsome, Daddy.

TODD: Where are we going?

JULIA: We're going to go home.

TODD: I want to go to the lake.

JULIA: I know, Dad.

YOUNG ALTHEA: Where was this lake?

JULIA: I don't really remember. He sold the place after my mother died.

YOUNG ALTHEA: That's too bad. When they let you go, that would have been a nice place to take him.

She regards Young Althea. It was a very kind thing to say.

JULIA: I'll take him somewhere else with a lake. He won't know.

TODD: The lake.

JULIA: Stay still, Dad.

Stephen enters, takes in the scene. Young Althea jumps up from her cot. Stephen holds his hand up to calm her.

YOUNG ALTHEA: I —

STEPHEN: (*to Young Althea*) It's fine. (*to Julia*) He was getting kind of scruffy.

JULIA: Look at him now.

STEPHEN: How is he feeling this morning?

JULIA: He's fine.

STEPHEN: How are you, Mr. Todd?

TODD: We're going to the lake.

STEPHEN: Oh, that'll be nice. (*to Julia*) You missed a spot. (*to Todd*) Would you like to have a visitor?

TODD: Bring them for afternoon toast and coffee.

STEPHEN: Bring who?

TODD: Heh?

STEPHEN: I hear everything you say, Mathias.

TODD: Toast and coffee, then. For the neighbours.

STEPHEN: No, it's someone else. A nice psychiatrist.

JULIA: For what?

STEPHEN: She's going to ask your father some questions.

JULIA: You mean you're having someone friendly to your cause create some data for you.

STEPHEN: No. This is about the *truth*, Miss Todd. But upstairs, they seem to need a little something to help them make up their minds. About your father's fitness. They don't think he can tell right from wrong! Isn't that funny?

JULIA: I want someone to see what's going on down here.

STEPHEN: Go. There's a nice judge up there who just told me to do whatever I need to do.

JULIA: We'll see how this judge feels about you torturing a prisoner.

She leaves to find someone.

TODD: Margaret?

YOUNG ALTHEA: Mr. Part? Should we wait?

STEPHEN: You have your orders, you'll do as you're told. Won't you?

YOUNG ALTHEA: Yes, Sir.

The lights change. Todd is the focus. A female VOICE (spoken by Young Althea) plays over the scene. Michael walks very slowly into the scene as it plays – riveted by Todd.

SONG: '*Oh Yasna*' (Ukrainian)

> *Oh Yasna zhe krasna*
> *De sonetchko shodyt*
> *a nyzenko zahodyt*
>> (The sky is turning red, where the sun is setting,
>> a married man is in love with a young girl)

VOICE: What is your name.

TODD: Todd. Mathias.

VOICE: What colour is a red apple.

TODD: Red.

VOICE: What colour is a banana.

TODD: There is something in apples that makes my mouth dry.

VOICE: Yellow. What colour is a banana.

TODD: Yellow.

VOICE: Bananas come in groups or bunches.

TODD: Who is this?

VOICE: Bunches. Answer. Bananas come in mobs or gangs.

TODD: Who is this?

VOICE: You are hungry. There is a restaurant nearby.

TODD: I'm hungry?

VOICE: There is a restaurant nearby. Is it acceptable for you to go and eat in the restaurant.

TODD: I can go in the restaurant?

VOICE: Do you wish to?

TODD: Yes.

VOICE: You are hungry. There is nowhere to eat.

TODD: I am going to have a bowl of soup and some farmers'
bread, Margaret.

VOICE: There is nowhere to eat.

TODD: Oh.

VOICE: You see a man with a roasted chicken. Is it acceptable for
you to take the man's roasted chicken.

TODD: Who is he?

VOICE: Answer the question.

TODD: But who is he?

VOICE: Is it acceptable for you to take the man's roasted chicken.

TODD: How big is the man? (*He laughs.*)

VOICE: You are in a lifeboat in a body of water.

TODD: It is a lake.

*Todd stands. He is in another reality now – remembering. The
doctor's voice recedes.*

VOICE: A ship is sinking and the lifeboat is almost full. There is
room for one woman from your country, or three children
who are foreigners.

TODD: (*to Michael*) There was a gazebo in the back of the house, which looked into the trees.

VOICE: She is a woman you know – a good woman, a neighbour.

MICHAEL: Who do you save, Mathias?

TODD: When they bought the land behind us, they cut all the trees. So it was as if I was the hermit living in the back of *their* land.

VOICE: The ship is sinking!

TODD: Can you imagine?

MICHAEL: Hey! Who do you kill? ANSWER THE QUES-TION.

TODD: My trees fall as if they've been infected.

VOICE: I've moved in behind you. I'm young and very beautiful.

TODD: How do they afford this land?

VOICE: I come and visit you in the gazebo, where sometimes you take the paper and a cup of coffee.

The lights are changing again.

VOICE: You've never seen eyes like mine.

TODD: Green.

VOICE: Silken hair. You said I had the hands of a violinist.

The voice is Young Althea's, who now comes into the scene as Helena Sonnen.

HELENA (YOUNG ALTHEA): I'm Helena Sonnen.

TODD: I know who you are. What do you want?

HELENA: I thought we could talk. We're neighbours. Neighbours talk.

Michael looks to Althea.

ALTHEA: The woman he killed.

MICHAEL: Yes.

ALTHEA: He relived this. Every night.

MICHAEL: Helena Sonnen.

HELENA: I brought you and your wife a bottle of plum wine. I made it last fall.

TODD: Oh. Thank you. I didn't realize your property had plum trees, too.

HELENA: It doesn't. They're your plums.

Despite himself, Todd laughs. She is quite something.

HELENA: We are going to be neighbours, Mr. Todd. Whether you're ready for me or not.

MICHAEL: Love just changes some people for the worse.

ALTHEA: That's your position, is it?

HELENA: We used to have nothing, Mr. Todd. I don't mean we had enough but we wanted more, I mean we had nothing. Is this seat taken?

MICHAEL: I remember when I met her …

JOANNA (JULIA): (*to Michael*) Is this seat taken?

SONG: '*Yonana*' (Zimbabwean)

> *This song is heard indistinctly in the background – as if it is party music being played in another room.*

MICHAEL: I was at a party and I was going to leave and go home. But someone poured some more wine into my glass and I stayed a little longer. And she came in around midnight. I would have been home if that person hadn't filled my glass. I would never have met her.

JOANNA: Is there any more of that?

TODD: The future should have come more slowly than it has, Miss Sonnen. Then we could all get used to it.

MICHAEL: I would have been home if that person hadn't filled my glass. I would never have met you.

HELENA: Well …

HELENA AND JOANNA: I just wanted to introduce myself.

TODD: Yes.

MICHAEL: Yes.

JOANNA: Joanna.

MICHAEL: (*Beat.*) Michael. (*They shake.*)

HELENA: Help you put a face to a name.

> *Todd and Young Althea shake hands in the background.*

MICHAEL: If I'd gone home, neither of us would ever have suffered.

JOANNA: You'd never have loved me, either.

MICHAEL: You wouldn't be with Colin.

JOANNA: (*affectionate*) I'm not with Colin because you stayed an extra hour at a party, you dope. I'm with him because I love him.

The party music ends. The women recede.

TODD: (*to Michael*) An excess of love.

MICHAEL: How can there be such a thing?   ·

We are back in the interrogation – 'Oh Yasna' once again heard under the following.

VOICE (YOUNG ALTHEA): Your daughter is starving.

JULIA: You should never have been allowed in here.

STEPHEN: It's not up to you to set the course of justice. Your people had their turn at the wheel.

VOICE: A family across the road from you has food.

JULIA: What's right is always right. And this is not right.

STEPHEN: Should we rely on *your* definition of what is right? What is good? What if what is good for *you* is bad for *me*? What if I have to die for *your* good?

VOICE: Is it acceptable to cross the road and take that other family's food.

TODD: Kill the others.

Silence.

STEPHEN: I beg your pardon?

TODD: Protect your tribe.

JULIA: He could be thinking of anything, Mr. Part.

STEPHEN: He knows.

VOICE: Their child is starving, but you have food.

JULIA: You just see what you want to see.

STEPHEN: Listen to him. You claimed you were interested in the truth, so why don't you listen?

VOICE: They come over and try to steal your food. You should kill them!

TODD: (*seeing Julia*) No ...

STEPHEN: Go on, Mathias, they're coming into your house.

TODD: I share my bread with them.

STEPHEN: (*going to the cell*) They're going rape your wife and child.

JULIA: (*to Stephen*) You bastard.

TODD: Go to the edge of town, wait until dark.

STEPHEN: They'll take them away from you!

TODD: I pray for them.

STEPHEN: They shoot your wife dead because you stuck your dick in one of them.

TODD: LEAVE US ALONE! I did nothing! Margaret! ... Julia!

JULIA: Dad, I'm right here.

TODD: (*Sees her. Quietly:*) I want to go back to Geneva. Take me home!

STEPHEN: Say that again.

MICHAEL: What did he say?

ALTHEA: Listen.

Young Althea returns.

YOUNG ALTHEA: You have to stop now, Mr. Part.

STEPHEN: (*of Todd*) What did he just say?

JULIA: Is anyone coming down?

YOUNG ALTHEA: No.

STEPHEN: He knows where he is! He shouldn't know where he is!

JULIA: He doesn't know anything.

STEPHEN: (*to Todd*) Let's continue, Mathias, where were we? Helena's people have come to kill your wife. Right in front of you. They've just come from Helena's house. They've learned that you have soiled Helena – you've left your seed in her!

YOUNG ALTHEA: Mr. Part, I have to inform you –

STEPHEN: And now they come to put you in your place. Yes, *you* in *your* place. They stand in your doorway and say to Margaret, 'Do you know what he has done?' They put a gun to her head and say to you, 'Tell her what you've done' –

JULIA: My mother was *murdered*, and you will use that –

STEPHEN: I will use anything –

JULIA: You are a monster.

STEPHEN: He is the monster.

YOUNG ALTHEA: Mr. Part, you have to leave the cells now.

STEPHEN: (*considering her*) Why?

YOUNG ALTHEA: They would like to see you upstairs.

STEPHEN: I will be up when I'm finished down here.

YOUNG ALTHEA: You are.

STEPHEN: (*Beat.*) What have you done. What did you say to them? (*of Todd and Julia*) These people got to you, didn't they? With their sob stories! (*He grabs Julia's face in his hand.*) Because: how could this face lie?

MICHAEL: Don't touch her –

JULIA: (*Shakes him off*) Get off me –

STEPHEN: She got under your skin.

YOUNG ALTHEA: She has nothing to do with it. Please go.

STEPHEN: I always knew you'd let us down.

He gets ready to leave, but returns partway and leans in to Todd.

STEPHEN: You put a pitchfork through your past and your future, Mathias.

He leaves. Silence.

JULIA: My god. Thank you for doing that.

YOUNG ALTHEA: I didn't do *anything* for you.

JULIA: Well, whatever you –

YOUNG ALTHEA: It's over now.

JULIA: I'm grateful.

YOUNG ALTHEA: No, it's *over*.

She produces a sheet of paper and hands it to Julia. Julia reads it and covers her mouth. Julia rushes to her father and shows him the letter.

JULIA: Dad? Look … the prisoner …. is released from the court's custody by order of the presiding judge … do you know what that means? We can go!

TODD: (*very emotional*) Helena?

JULIA: What?

TODD: Helena.

JULIA: (*to Althea*) Do you see? What all of this confusion has done to him? (*to Todd*) I'm taking you home, Dad.

MICHAEL: Did you intercede on her behalf?

ALTHEA: You're the expert on offstage events, you tell me.

MICHAEL: (*looking at the scene*) I think you did. You came to your senses. You did the right thing.

ALTHEA: Does that make you feel better? To think of me as a good person?

Michael doesn't answer.

YOUNG ALTHEA: The bailiff will be down with his belongings. You sign a release form, and then you can go.

JULIA: Things are going to turn out all right for you, Althea. You'll see.

ALTHEA: (*looking at Julia*) She has five minutes to live.

MICHAEL: I don't believe you.

ALTHEA: You don't want to believe me.

MICHAEL: If it was true, you'd dread telling it to me. But I understand what you're doing. You want to teach me a lesson.

ALTHEA: What makes you think this isn't the part of the story I like?

Michael is stopped in his tracks, realizing what she's saying.

Now she has four minutes.

Footsteps.

JULIA: Come on, Daddy. Here's the bailiff. Meet your last visitor.

But it is Stephen. He looks stricken standing before them as Julia brings her father out of the cell. As Michael listens to the following, it is as if the characters are suspended in time – speaking their lines straight out. The belongings Stephen throws at Mathias will be mimed – although we will hear them hitting Mathias.

STEPHEN: I brought his belongings.

MICHAEL: Althea …

ALTHEA: No. This is what happened.

YOUNG ALTHEA: Mr. Part. You shouldn't be down here now.

STEPHEN: I am in the employ of the court.

JULIA: Give me his things.

STEPHEN: I suppose he'll live out his days in peace now.

JULIA: As he should. You have no idea the damage you've done.

STEPHEN: I do. It is not to him I've done it, though. (*He mimes reaching into a bag. Removes a wallet, which he throws at Todd.*) Wallet. With all your identification.

YOUNG ALTHEA: Mr. Part, I'm going to have to get security.

STEPHEN: Certainly! Go get our brothers.

JULIA: (*to Althea*) No – don't go anywhere.

STEPHEN: (*Takes a set of keys out of the bag, throws them at Todd.*) Keys. To get into your villa. Lots of keys for a man who can't remember much. (*to Julia*) Your father can never be tried now, no matter what. (*to Todd*) *Non compos mentis*. But we know that you *are* competent, papa. Very. (*Takes a lighter out of the bag, throws it.*) Lighter.

ALTHEA: I'm a witness to all of this.

STEPHEN: (*rounding on Althea and Michael*) A *witness*? Did I hear you right? A witness? (*to Young Althea*) I wonder what your parents would make of you now. Or your Domenic. (*She can't or won't respond. He turns to Julia.*) He said he wanted to go home. To Geneva.

JULIA: So what. We've lived there for more than ten years. He knows where he lives.

STEPHEN: He said *to* Geneva. He knows he's not there now.

TODD: Geneva.

STEPHEN: Yes, exactly.

YOUNG ALTHEA: He did say that. (*Something begins to change in Young Althea – a growing suspicion.*)

STEPHEN: (*Reaches into bag, throws a handful of coins at Todd, which clatter onto the ground.*) Pocket change. You didn't think it through, Mathias. If you had Alzheimer's, you wouldn't know you'd ever left Geneva. We could send you over Niagara Falls in a barrel and you'd still think you were in Switzerland. You'd never ask to *go* back.

JULIA: That's your proof?

STEPHEN: You think I didn't do my research? I'm GOOD. But I applaud you both – you've fulfilled your destiny: you win. Geneva, yes?

JULIA: Stephen – this is ridiculous.

TODD: Helena?

STEPHEN: Whatever. You're free to go, but I want you to look your daughter in the eye and tell her you've lied to her. About everything.

TODD: I know him.

STEPHEN: Stop it now. All you have to do is say, 'Julia, there's not a thing wrong with me, and, by the way, I might have left out a detail or two about what I was doing during our little genocide.' Just say it. Then you can go.

TODD: Where?

STEPHEN: I said stop it, Mathias. (*He holds up his hand, and, as he speaks the next word, it takes on the shape of a pistol.*) Pistol.

Stephen turns the mimed gun on Julia. The scene explodes into a tense naturalism.

JULIA: He didn't have a gun!

STEPHEN: But he still has a mouth.

JULIA: My god ... Althea?

MICHAEL: A gun?

ALTHEA: He smuggled it in.

STEPHEN: Tell her, Mathias. So everyone knows.

JULIA: No one could act this well, Stephen, and you know it.

STEPHEN: Aren't you the least bit curious? Don't you want to know what he has done?

JULIA: Go on then, Dad. Tell me everything.

TODD: What does he want to hear?

JULIA: That you're a murderer and a man who hates in his heart.

TODD: (*seeing the gun*) What are they doing here?

STEPHEN: I'm warning you, Mathias. I've got nothing to lose now.

TODD: (*turning to Julia*) Margaret, go wait for me in the library.

JULIA: (*to Stephen*) Are you listening?

STEPHEN: Say it.

TODD: He wants me to tell you the truth.

JULIA: Stephen, you've convinced yourself –

STEPHEN: I'm waiting –

JULIA: Your people will understand you tried –

STEPHEN: SHUT UP.

JULIA: Althea?

YOUNG ALTHEA: (*coldly*) Listen to what he's saying.

He moves in closer to them.

STEPHEN: All right, Mathias. We're *all* listening now. You tell her everything, or I'll shoot her. I will pull this trigger.

TODD: Wait. (*A pause. Then, to Julia*) I … fell in love.

STEPHEN: I'm counting to three.

MICHAEL: What's wrong with you? You're just standing there.

ALTHEA: He began to count.

STEPHEN: One –

TODD: There was a woman.

MICHAEL: You didn't do anything?

ALTHEA: I did. I watched.

STEPHEN: Say the number! Half a million!

TODD: I know I've ruined your happiness. Please forgive me.

STEPHEN: Two –

TODD: My wife's done nothing to you! Please don't. (*He begins to weep.*) Don't hurt her. I love her. Don't hurt her.

JULIA: (*Certainty dawns.*) You're going to shoot whether he answers you or not.

Stephen makes a threatening gesture.

MICHAEL: STOP!

The scene freezes and is silent but for the sound of Todd weeping.

JULIA: Stop? Why? (*She turns to Michael.*) Are you going to rescue me?

MICHAEL: He's going to –

JULIA: What, Michael? What's he going to do?

MICHAEL: You know what he's going to do.

JULIA: It's a bit late for things to end differently.

MICHAEL: Please don't say that.

JULIA: This is what happened.

STEPHEN: SAY IT!

JULIA: (*to Todd*) Don't tell him anything. (*to Michael*) It's going to be such a relief to be free of you.

STEPHEN: Tell her the truth, or so help me –

MICHAEL: Three.

Instant blackout, gunshot. Lights up, Michael is stunned speechless. Todd holds the lifeless body of his daughter.

SONG: '*Dejgidi*' (Macedonian)

The song runs quietly under the following scene.

Dejgidi ludi mladi godini
Dejgidi ludi mladi godini
     (O you wild years of youth)
Letnavte kako sivi galabi
Letnavte kako sivi galabi
     (You flew away like grey doves)

TODD: Margaret? Margaret …

STEPHEN: You fucking *monster* – Say her name! Julia! How can you keep this up? Julia!

TODD: Julia.

STEPHEN: *Yes*! Julia! Your daughter!

TODD: Where's Margaret?

STEPHEN: God. No, no –

YALTHEA: Please, Stephen! Go! Give me the gun and go.

Stephen is stunned, frozen. He realizes what he has done. Young Althea mimes taking the gun from him.

YOUNG ALTHEA: Stephen – GO!

Stephen exits.

TODD: Julia … ?

YOUNG ALTHEA: (*She goes very close to Mathias.*) How does it feel? You remember this, Mathias. You remember this. (*She smashes him with the gun and he collapses.*) I want you to remember THIS.

ALTHEA: They caught Stephen.

MICHAEL: (*still in a kind of horrified dream*) Stephen?

ALTHEA: Yes, Stephen.

MICHAEL: And what did they do with you?

ALTHEA: They caught Stephen. Before the sun went down.

MICHAEL: (*Beat.*) What happened to him?

ALTHEA: Nothing. They never found the murder weapon. Or a witness to testify.

Young Althea holds up the pistol. She produces a real cloth and mimes cleaning the gun, then hides it on her person.

ALTHEA: So they let him go.

Young Althea looks at Michael.

ALTHEA: What would you have done?

MICHAEL: I ... I don't know.

YOUNG ALTHEA: Now you've made some progress.

They are now back in her drawing room. Julia's body is between them.

MICHAEL: (*to us*) I had a moment then. Something came to me, like the ringing of a bell: a clear, bright sound in my mind. The man in the bar.

STEPHEN: Oh, I like you. You take it all so personally!

MICHAEL: He saw right through me.

STEPHEN: You'd be a fool to turn down your only opportunity to have your question answered. (*Michael looks at Stephen, whom he now realizes was the man he met in the bar across the street.*) Why do good people rush to do evil ... And what do they become?

MICHAEL: Stephen Part. (*Beat.*) Jesus, how long has he been sitting there? Waiting for someone to ... You still have it.

ALTHEA: No.

MICHAEL: You do.

ALTHEA: (*Laughs bitterly.*) That gun is proof of his guilt.

MICHAEL: He knows. Without it he can't ... (*dawning*) He'll never be –

ALTHEA: (*Laughs.*) You know why he picked you? He wanted you to see what you were going to turn into.

MICHAEL: No.

ALTHEA: A lonesome fuck-up who can't live with what he's done.

MICHAEL: No. No. No ... You have to go see him, Althea. Get up! He must still be there!

ALTHEA: I'm not going any –

He reaches for her and she pulls away – this becomes a sort of struggle as he tries to pull her to her feet, and we see for the first time how terrified Althea is of leaving her apartment.

ALTHEA: LET GO OF ME.

He does.

MICHAEL: You can't sit here forever. You need to ...

ALTHEA: To mend your broken soul, Althea? To get some closure, Althea? Poor Althea! What are you to me? Where were you with your notebook when we needed a witness? Bathing in milk and writing cheques for charity, that's where you were: one dollar a day – buy a village a goat. Meanwhile they beat their ploughshares back into swords and left our children butchered on the ground. So now I cross the road and you make it all better? Or have you figured out a way I can go back and be born somewhere else?

MICHAEL: It doesn't matter. You'd still find a way to lose everything and then lie here in the dark, steeping in your own sick. That's the life you made for yourself. It's no one's fault but yours.

She stares at him a moment in silent rage and then gets up out of her chair, goes off and retrieves the cloth that Young Althea is still holding.

ALTHEA: Is this what you want? (*She unwraps the cloth and holds up a real gun.*) Go on, take it.

She holds it out and he looks at it.

ALTHEA: (*roaring at him*) TAKE IT.

He does. Stares at it in his hand.

ALTHEA: How does that feel?

MICHAEL: You're no better than they were.

ALTHEA: You still believe that because a person suffers, they must be good? Because you suffer well, you think God will reward you with justice? I settled for less, and Stephen Part settled for less, and you're going to settle for less when your time comes. Because your wailing won't bring back your dead, and you'll have to do *something*.

MICHAEL: (*Hands the gun out to her.*) Take this to him. It's not me he wants. Go back to the world of human beings.

ALTHEA: Where you come from? No thank you.

MICHAEL: It must have taken him years to find you. Doesn't that count for something?

ALTHEA: No. I've done my part. You keep that thing. Give it to him if you want. Or take it home. Pick it up any time you think you can make a better world.

Althea watches him. He takes it to himself.

SONG: 'Binaya' (Central West African)

Young Althea sings quietly in the background. She is joined by the others.
Binaya la bis stobu sala daneh bifoghu
Binaya mashi mashi hu sala daneh bifighu
Binaya Binaya Binaya Binaya

ALTHEA: Now you give something in exchange. Spiritual collateral.

She holds her hand out. For a moment, he's not sure what she means, but then it lands. He passes her the notebook and she opens it and looks inside, then closes the cover and holds the book at her side.

ALTHEA: Now we're back where we started. I'm harmless and you know nothing. I've turned back time.

MICHAEL: Althea –

ALTHEA: No.

Song ends abruptly.

Michael looks at her, waiting, but nothing is going to change. He leaves the apartment.

MICHAEL: I went down the stairs alone to the street and stood under her window across from the bar. I could feel the gun in my pocket, a cold, dark weight. There is a question I never know how to answer.

TODD: How does it feel?

MICHAEL: How does what feel? To be left? To be the last of anything? To be trapped inside of THIS, not knowing what it would be like to be anything else?

I thought of going back into the bar, to see if he was still there. But then I … threw the gun into the trash. And I ran. After a couple of blocks, I flagged a cab, said, 'Heathrow.'

As Michael speaks the following, the cast slowly assembles upstage.

It was evening, I was being driven away from that place where Althea and Stephen Part were never going to meet, and the street was filling with people, people going home, going out. Going to the movies. To the theatre. To be with each other. In groups. In gangs.

Michael points the gun, which he is still holding, at Althea, maybe at some of the other characters, maybe himself, and maybe at the audience. Or maybe he just stares at it for a moment, weighing it.

How does it feel to be out there in the dark? Just watching. Invisible, but still a part of everything. A part of *this*. How does that feel?

Althea turns to look at Michael and begins to sing, as if in answer to his question. The cast joins the song, as does Michael, slowly lowering the gun, drawn to Althea. All then walk towards the audience. The song stops one note short of completion.

SONG: '*Tobela*' (Zimbabwean)

Horiyatsa	(Look around / pay attention)
Hamuzani waka	(To what is happening)
Tobela	(Pray)
Ayitobela Murena	(O Pray to God)

Chorus:
Tobela Murena / Tobela Murena
Tobela Murena / Tobela Murena

Horiyatsa	(Look around / pay attention)
Hamuzani waka	(To what is happening)

Tobela	(Pray)
Ayitobela Murena	(O Pray to God)
Iyo-o / Iyo-o / Iyo-o	(a soothing sound)
Ayitobela Murena	(O Pray to God)
Horiyatsa	(Look around / pay attention)
Hamuzani waka	(To what is happening)
Tobela	(Pray)
Ayitobela –	(O pray to –)

Silence. The cast stands downstage facing the audience. Michael holds the gun in his hand. He looks down at it. Beat. He looks up at the audience.

Long beat.

Blackout.

On the production and this text

Goodness is my second collaboration with Ross Manson and Volcano. The first, *Building Jerusalem*, opened in 2000 after four years of workshopping, revision and fruitful agony. In 2003, during one of our regular creative catch-ups, Ross revealed he'd been doing research in the field of moral philosophy (the study of ethics), and I admitted that I had the bare bones for a play about a war criminal with Alzheimer's. We took our two notions to Blyth in the summer of 2003, and with the help of six actors, banged them together to see if they would turn into a play. They did.

Two years later, on October 25, 2005, *Goodness* had its world premiere at Toronto's Tarragon Theatre, as a Volcano/Tarragon co-production. This book went to press on October 20 and I was forbidden from coming within two hundred metres of Coach House Press as of October 18. It was a sound policy.

This means that minor, last-minute changes made within the final week before opening may not be reflected in here. Openings and publication dates provide a useful barrier to further revisions. So here is the play, to the best of my knowledge. One note for future productions is that, at the end of the last scene with Michael and Althea, I had written that Althea would destroy the notebook. Obviously, this changes the temperature of that scene significantly. For the Volcano/Tarragon production, we thought it was equally potent for her to take it and keep it, and this decision is reflected in the printed version of the script. Future productions may wish to experiment with the alternate resolution.

Details about the stage design have been omitted from this text, as future productions may find it useful to wrestle in their own way with the play's casual disregard for time and space. But the original production featured eight chairs around the periphery of a spare room designed by Teresa Przybylski that functioned both as an understairs holding pen and as Althea's dark, quiet one-bedroom apartment in London. Rebecca Picherack's lighting design further created spaces within this space—by the time the production opened, 72 lights had been hung and there were 120 individual lighting cues.

The music in this play was sourced and developed by Ross Manson and Brenna MacCrimmon, with the aid of Waleed Abdulhamid, Kitka, Teddy Masuku, Mariana Sadowska and Sarah Sanford. The placement as well as lyrics to all of the folk songs used in *Goodness* have been published here, but not the music itself. In some cases, such as with much of the African music, the lyrics are phonetical approximations of folk songs taught live to the cast by native speakers. My apologies to anyone who finds a typo in these lyrics; we did our best to render them faithfully. Most of the songs used in the original production were performed live by the actors and complemented by a gorgeous chiarascuro of a soundscape designed by John Gzowski. For guidance, future productions may wish to avail themselves of a CD recording of the music in this play, which is available from the author's agent (see the copyright page for that information).

Michael Redhill, October 18, 2005

Thank you

To Ross Manson for his commitment, his passion and the clarity of his theatrical vision, as well as all the actors who were involved at one stage or another in the development of the production: Leah Cherniak, Sean Dixon, Jerry Franken, John Fitzgerald Jay, Hardee Lineham, Soheil Parsa, Jane Spidell, Ordena Stephens and Sanjay Talwar. My gratitude goes especially to Tom Barnett, Sarah Sanford and Karen Robinson, who originated the parts, respectively, of Stephen, Julia and Althea. Fate decreed they could not join us for the world premiere, but the fibre of these three characters owe a great deal to the presences of these three actors in the creative process. To Victor Ertmanis, Tara Hughes and Jordan Pettle I owe a similarly profound debt, but I also have the pleasure of seeing them in the final production. Stepping in and taking over from Tom, Sarah and Karen were Jack Nicholsen, Bernadeta Wrobel and Lili Francks, each of whom plunged into a madly rushing river, picked up the paddles and kept going with grace and aplomb. My thanks to them for their talent and their faith in this play. Thanks as well to JP Robichaud, who stage-managed and is the invisible master of everything.

Many thanks to Richard Rose and everyone at Tarragon, for their enthusiasm and support, and everyone at Volcano who is not Ross Manson, namely producer Camilla Holland and associate artistic director Lara Azzopardi. Finally, my thanks to Alana Wilcox, Rick/Simon and the sleepless pressmen at Coach House Books, for putting themselves through a ridiculous schedule.

MICHAEL REDHILL is the publisher and one of the editors of *Brick, A Literary Journal*. His most recent books are *Fidelity*, a collection of short fiction; *Martin Sloane*, a novel that was nominated for the Giller Prize, the Trillium Award, the Torgi Award, the City of Toronto Book Award, the Books in Canada/Amazon Best First Novel Prize and won the Commonwealth Prize for Best First Book; *Light-crossing*, a collection of poetry; and *Building Jerusalem*, a play, which won a Dora for Best New Play and a Chalmers Award for Playwriting and was nominated for a Governor General's Award. His new novel, *Consolation*, will be published in fall 2006. He lives with his partner and two sons in Toronto.

Typeset in Janson
Printed and bound at the Coach House on bpNichol Lane, 2005

Edited and designed by Alana Wilcox
Cover by Rick/Simon
Author photo by Kevin Kelly

Coach House Books
401 Huron Street on bpNichol Lane
Toronto, Ontario
M5S 2G5

416 979 2217
800 367 6360

mail@chbooks.com
www.chbooks.com